More Praise for *What to Do When*

"Stack's incredible book shows you ho. get more done faster than you ever thought possible."
—**Brian Tracy, author of *Eat That Frog!* and *No Excuses!***

"This book will save you time, money, and—most of all—your sanity. In our fast-moving, multitasking world of now-now-now, Laura Stack is an extraordinary resource for you, and her expertise is delivered with this book."
—**Tim Sanders, bestselling author and former Chief Solutions Officer, Yahoo!**

"I don't know anybody who is more organized or who has more energy and has more fun getting things done than Laura Stack. No kidding. She doesn't just write about what she knows; she writes about what she lives. If you feel like there's too much to do, read this book for tips, tactics, and strategies that will decrease the time you invest and increase the results you enjoy."
—**Mark Sanborn, author of *Up, Down, or Sideways* and *The Fred Factor***

"Laura's Productivity Workflow Formula will help you become the 5 percent employee that creates 95 percent of the company's value. Yet another high-value tool from the Productivity Pro!"
—**Jeff Bettinger, Chief Career Strategist, HelpMyResume.com**

"I am a raving fan of Laura Stack because she is the absolute master of teaching me how to do less and achieve more. For me, like so many others, time has become the new currency. I can always make more money, but I can't make more time. Laura teaches me to make much better use of the time that I have so that I can do more of what I want to do. For me, that's priceless. This book will motivate you to do the simple yet powerful things that can make your work and your life immeasurably more productive and fulfilling."
—**Joe Calloway, author of *Becoming a Category of One***

"Leadership, strategy, and business acumen are essential for being successful in business today. At the heart of Laura's effective productivity system are strategies to maximize these essential business skills. Read this book! Adopting her system will unleash your strategic thinking potential and productivity in your business and maximize your results. It has worked for us, and I guarantee it will work for you!"
—**Mike Howard, Chief Security Officer, Microsoft Corporation**

"In this prolific and pragmatic guide, you will find tangible strategies for tackling the working world's toughest issue: time management. Finally, someone has realized we're at maximum capacity, and Stack gives us usable ideas to help us reduce, reduce, reduce."

—**Rory Vaden, cofounder, Southwestern Consulting, and *New York Times* bestselling author of *Take the Stairs***

"If you have so much to do that you're not sure what to do, here's the first thing to do: buy Laura's book!"

—**Randy Gage, author of *Prosperity Mind***

"Are you overworked, overstressed, and overwhelmed, yet still you're underproducing? Laura Stack can help you. Buy this book and devour it. You can do less, stress less, and still achieve more. It's possible! Learn how inside."

—**Darren Hardy, Publisher, *Success* magazine, and *New York Times* bestselling author of *The Compound Effect***

"Laura Stack is an extraordinary teacher, speaker, and coach who inspires people to become peak performers. This book is a must-read for anyone who wants to stop 'doing more with less' but 'do less to achieve more.'"

—**Dr. Nido R. Qubein, President, High Point University, and Chairman, Great Harvest Bread Company**

"Laura Stack improved our work flow, communication, coordination, documentation support, and teamwork. Her touch to our business made and continues to make a lasting change for the better. I can't say enough about how helpful her knowledge and training have been."

—**Montague Boyd, Senior Vice President, Investments, UBS Financial Services**

"Counterbalancing my practice that 'If you aren't overwhelmed, you're not reaching your greatest productivity' is Laura Stack's most logical advice found in her latest book. Laura's philosophy is that what you opt *not* to do is often as important as—and often more important than—what you *do*. This book is all about productivity and making the most of the time that we all find in such short supply. Take the time to read the book, and you'll amaze yourself at the demonstrated and proven results."

—**Tim Jackson, CAE, CMP, President and CEO, Colorado Automobile Dealers Association**

WHAT TO DO WHEN THERE'S **TOO MUCH** TO DO

Reduce Tasks, Increase Results,
and Save 90 Minutes a Day

LAURA STACK

BK

Berrett–Koehler Publishers, Inc.
San Francisco
a BK Life book

Berrett-Koehler Publishers, Inc.
235 Montgomery Street, Suite 650
San Francisco, CA 94104-2916
Tel: (415) 288-0260 Fax: (415) 362-2512 www.bkconnection.com

Ordering Information

Quantity sales. Special discounts are available on quantity purchases by corporations, associations, and others. For details, contact the "Special Sales Department" at the Berrett-Koehler address above.
Individual sales. Berrett-Koehler publications are available through most bookstores. They can also be ordered directly from Berrett-Koehler: Tel: (800) 929-2929; Fax: (802) 864-7626; www.bkconnection.com
Orders for college textbook/course adoption use. Please contact Berrett-Koehler: Tel: (800) 929-2929; Fax: (802) 864-7626.
Orders by U.S. trade bookstores and wholesalers. Please contact Ingram Publisher Services, Tel: (800) 509-4887; Fax: (800) 838-1149; E-mail: customer.service@ingrampublisherservices.com; or visit www.ingrampublisherservices.com/Ordering for details about electronic ordering.

Berrett-Koehler and the BK logo are registered trademarks of Berrett-Koehler Publishers, Inc.

Text design by Yvonne Tsang at Wilsted & Taylor Publishing Services
Cover design by Pemastudio
Printed in the United States of America

Berrett-Koehler books are printed on long-lasting acid-free paper. When it is available, we choose paper that has been manufactured by environmentally responsible processes. These may include using trees grown in sustainable forests, incorporating recycled paper, minimizing chlorine in bleaching, or recycling the energy produced at the paper mill.

Library of Congress Cataloging-in-Publication Data
Stack, Laura.
What to do when there's too much to do : reduce tasks, increase results, and save 90 minutes a day / Laura Stack. — 1st ed.
p. cm.
Includes bibliographical references and index.
ISBN 978-1-60994-539-8 (pbk.)
1. Time management.   2. Work-life balance.   I. Title.
HD69.T54S7284 2012
650.1'1—dc23   2012006636

First Edition
17 16 15 14 13 12   10 9 8 7 6 5 4 3 2 1

To my son,

JAMES STACK

When I have too much to do,
spending time with you
puts life in perspective and
makes everything better.
I love you.

CONTENTS

PREFACE

One morning, as I entered a ballroom to deliver a keynote address for a Fortune 100 telecommunications company, one of the employees approached me. She didn't look happy. "I have to tell you something," she said. "I'm not excited about you being here."

I was a bit taken aback, since I hadn't even opened my mouth yet. "No kidding," I replied. "Do you mind telling me why?"

"Absolutely," she continued. "I have no desire to be more productive. I'm working as hard as I possibly can. I'm killing myself with twelve-hour days and already have way too much to do. I don't want a productivity consultant telling me to do more with less. I want to do less and achieve more."

The lightbulb went on, and I reassured her, "That's exactly what I'm here to help you do."

I established my company, The Productivity Pro®, Inc., in 1992 to help people achieve Maximum Results in Minimum Time®. This woman's description of "too much to do" and desire to "do less and achieve more" framed my twenty-year mission perfectly and inspired the title of this book.

Frankly, doing more isn't always better. Would your manager be more impressed if you completed thirty-seven low-value tasks in one day, or just seven tasks with incredible impact? Can an eight-hour-a-day employee be more productive than a twelve-hour-a-day employee? You know the answers. What really matters is *results*—not check marks—and not hours. Busyness doesn't necessarily equal productivity, no matter how you slice it. No one really cares how many hours you were in the building or if you finished your to-do list.

People only care about what you're able to produce and the value of those results.

I wrote this book to help you achieve more *impactful* results, not necessarily *more* results. I also realize the irony of asking you to spend some of your precious time reading this book, given all you already have on your plate. But all worthwhile things take time to implement, so I urge you to consider this an investment toward greater time-savings in the future.

We'll focus on doing less and achieving more, not doing more with less—thus the subtitle, "Reduce Tasks, Increase Results, and Save 90 Minutes a Day." The promise of this book is to be a hero at work and get a life at the same time. It's good for you, because your results will be stellar, and you'll achieve greater life balance. It's good for your employer, because you won't leave your company to search for a better life. Your satisfaction and morale will increase, and your employer's turnover will decrease.

Productivity is a win-win scenario!

Doing less will require a reset of your default "Go, Go, Go!" setting. Today's fast-paced, high-pressure environment often requires sixty, seventy, eighty, or more hours a week. But productivity tends to decrease as work hours increase; after all, how can you perform at your best when you're overworked and constantly tired? You'll make more mistakes and spend more time fixing them. You'll get further behind and run faster to stay in one place. It's a vicious, overwhelming cycle, and for many people, it seems impossible to break.

But buying this book proves you're determined to try. Just stop for a minute and ask yourself: "Do I *really* need to work so long and hard to get everything done . . . or is it possible I'm being inefficient?" When you take an honest look at your daily habits, workflow, and processes, you may discover there's a clog in your productivity.

What to Do When There's Too Much to Do turns traditional time management on its head, because many old-fashioned techniques are meaningless for today's working professional.

When I started college in the late 1980s and attended my first time-management course, the instructor taught us to write down our schedules for the entire day, including the specific time we'd work on each task. I dutifully wrote up-to-the-minute agendas, detailing what I would do and when. From 8:00 to 8:30, I'll do this task. From 8:30 to 9:10, I'll do that task. Back then I could pretty much keep up with it, and my days usually went as planned. When something unexpected came up, it was fairly easy to adjust my agenda.

Then things started to change. Fax machines, voicemail, the Internet, e-mail, handhelds, apps, and all kinds of other technology exploded on the scene. The productivity game changed forever. Today, if you attempt to plan out every minute of your day, your schedule will blow up in the first five minutes.

With so much information and so much to do, it's become harder to be productive—and yet we feel busier than ever. With the recession, we're running lean and mean. We have greater expectations, fewer resources, and more work placed on us, which results in more time in the office and less time for life and loved ones.

Desperate workers are more stressed than ever before, as they receive information from multiple sources and attempt to track and organize it. We're constantly communicating with more people, more quickly, through more media, so we have more conversations to recall.

If you added up the amount of time it would take to complete the tasks on a typical person's to-do list, there might be hundreds of hours of work represented there. You can spend more time "planning" and "prioritizing" than just doing the work! Due to the blazing speed at which information flows, it's a waste of time to keep reordering a giant to-do list. Instead, organize your life around the stuff that really matters. Adopt a systematic workflow process to help you determine your high-value tasks, protect the time to do them, and focus on their execution.

If you've got far too much to do and desperately need to take back some of your time, know that it's possible to do so, assuming you're willing to put some sincere effort into the attempt. By following the logical, intuitive workflow process I present in this book, you can wrestle your schedule into submission. Ultimately, you can recover as much as ninety minutes of your day (or even more) to use as you see fit.

But before I launch into the details of this new and unique system, there are some people I'd like to acknowledge. I thank God for the gift of all these people in my life!

I want to thank my husband, John, who is my biggest fan and supporter. He puts up with my bizarre travel schedule and entrepreneurial lifestyle with understanding and cheerfulness. You have my undying gratitude and love.

Meagan, Johnny, and James, my children, I'm so proud to be your mom I could just burst.

Thanks to my incredible office manager, Becca Fletcher, my productivity weapon of choice. I am so fortunate to have you in my life and literally don't know what I'd do without you. Everyone needs a Becca!

I'm so grateful to Eileen Stack, my wonderful mother-in-law, who tirelessly helps our family and takes care of our children if both parents are out of town. Thank you for your unfailing love.

Mark and Darla Sanborn are great pals, and we have so much fun together. Spending time with you reminds me life's so much more than work!

I'm indebted to my mentor of eight years, Dianna Booher, CSP, CPAE, author of forty-five books, for the countless hours of time she's lovingly given me. I appreciate you introducing me to the team at Berrett-Koehler, who immediately believed in me and this book. Thanks to my editor, Neal Maillet, for your guidance throughout the project.

Thanks to my proofreader, Floyd Largent, for his eagle eyes and incredible editing skills.

I extend my heartfelt gratitude to our hundreds of clients, who have provided us the opportunity to work with you on the strategies in this book, learn from your feedback, see the results, and hear about your successes. Thanks for your enthusiastic support of my work.

I'm privileged to be the 2011–2012 president of the National Speakers Association. Over my nearly twenty years of membership, I've gained many wonderful friends, too many to mention by name, but you know who you are. Thank you for your encouragement, coaching, and camaraderie.

The Case for Reduction

If you're serious about your career, then you've probably read a number of books about time management and productivity in an effort to make better use of your workday. So what's new about this one? *What to Do When There's Too Much to Do* is unique in its approach to workflow, and I think you'll find it a breath of fresh air in an overcrowded and increasingly redundant field. Simply stated, the central message is *it's better to do less, not more, so you can do better, more focused work.*

Many workers find this a startling concept, because they increasingly have to work harder and longer with fewer resources—and that's precisely why my message is so very important. Over the last few decades we've learned to be superbly productive, yes, but in a way that can't be sustained over the long haul.

From a business perspective, productivity is the rate at which goods or services are produced per unit of labor. On a wider scale, this measure of corporate success is also a primary metric of the overall economic health of a nation. Collectively, we Americans are more productive today than at any time in our history.[1] But just think about the factors motivating this productivity increase, especially in recent years. Many businesses have cut their staffs to the bone in an effort to save the bottom line; as a result, the truncated workforce must somehow do more with less, just like the woman who stopped me before my presentation that day. We've defaulted to working long hours just so we can keep our jobs. And it's killing us.

In fact, I think we've just about hit the ceiling of what we can accomplish by stretching ourselves so thin we're practically transparent. Consider this worrisome factoid: According to a government report released in August 2011, American productivity declined for two consecutive quarters for the first time since 2008.[2] The second-quarter decline for 2011 was a bit less than expected: an annual adjusted rate of 0.7 percent rather than the anticipated 0.9 percent (yay?).[3] The bad news: 2011's first-quarter productivity figure, originally estimated at 1.8 percent growth, suffered a sharp downward revision to reflect an actual productivity *drop* of 0.6 percent.

Granted, we've experienced a minor economic expansion in the past few years. But the positive effects have been mostly limited to businesses, with very little trickle-down to individual workers. Indeed, as some observers have pointed out, many businesses posted productivity gains from early 2009 to late 2010 *only* because they had previously cut costs. In the process they pared down their workforces, requiring the workers they retained to work longer hours—often for the same compensation.

This refusal to increase the average worker's pay even while forcing them to work harder may seem draconian, and in one sense it is. Workers know that there are plenty of people lined up to take their jobs if they complain too much about the pay and long hours, and many employers press this fact to their advantage.

But in a larger sense, the flat compensation growth just continues a trend visible in the statistics since 1980. According to a study released by the *New York Times* in September 2011, compensation grew steadily along with American productivity from 1949 until 1979, and then more or less flattened out—even as productivity skyrocketed.[4] Productivity rose 80 percent from 1979 to 2009; compensation increased just 8 percent. That contrasts sharply with increases of 119 percent and 100 percent, respectively, in the 30 previous years. Basically, for the last three decades, American workers have been willing to accept insipid pay increases while pushing productivity through the roof.

But now we've hit the wall. As a class, we're exhausted, and any motivation to maximize productivity is mostly negative rather than positive. Recent economic growth may have been good for businesses, but it shortchanged the workers. We built on unstable economic ground . . . and now we're starting to see the cracks in the foundation. Even with high unemployment rates, employers complain about not being able to find competent workers.

SAVING OUR OWN LIVES

So today, I preach the gospel of ruthless task reduction, because I honestly believe an abandonment of unnecessary chores, and a drastic triage of all that remains, is the only way to be consistently, profitably productive in this economy without destroying your health, your family life, and your joy.

Many workers think that a willingness to do whatever it takes, at the expense of all else, can cure any workplace ailment. Their employers, and society at large, have trained them to think this way. But they never seem to understand a salient point here: you don't have to kill yourself to prove your dedication to the company and produce the tremendous results required.

And I mean exactly that. The Japanese have an entrenched tradition of working superhuman amounts of unpaid overtime, more to demonstrate company loyalty than to enhance productivity. It also drives high levels of *karoshi*, the practice of literally working yourself to death. This problem isn't unique to Japan; Westerners have the same problem, though our medical establishment doesn't really keep tabs on it as such.

Is the possibility of a raise or promotion really worth risking your health? And let me emphasize the word "possibility" —after all, how can you ensure your hard work is even registering with the higher-ups? You can't just try to outwork the other guy. Instead, get a handle on what's really important in your organization, and focus on aligning business strategy with your day-to-day execution. Don't just push and push and push until you can't go on anymore. Ironically, this can limit your usefulness to your company rather than increasing it.

HARSH REALITIES

Working too many hours is demonstrably counterproductive, because it results in decreased productivity. Studies have repeatedly shown that a sixty-hour workweek results, on average, in a 25 percent decrease in productivity.[5] The productivity numbers just get worse as the number of work hours increases, because exhaustion steadily erodes judgment and performance. Eventually, no matter how good your intentions, you hit a point of diminishing returns. If you go too far, your habits of overwork may harm your organization's bottom line—the exact opposite of what you intended when you set out on your quest to prove yourself.

The lesson here? You aren't a robot. Long hours lead to physical and mental fatigue, which results in slower work, more mistakes, and wasted time. It may also lead to depression, which can spiral out of control if left untreated—as is often the case, because the person affected is too busy to take care of it. Depression comes with harsh penalties of its own, and they can feed back into the productivity issues and make them even worse.

The old forty-hour workweek was originally struck as a compromise, as the best balance between productivity and overwork. Today, a forty-hour week isn't plausible for many people, given the expectations or structures of their jobs. Some people continue to insist they function better with a more demanding schedule. But they fail to recognize the signs of when they've reached capacity. Are you willing to do what it takes to short-circuit a drop in performance? You'd take good care of any other tool, wouldn't you? So why not take care of yourself?

THE SOLUTION

In the next six chapters, I'll show you how to train yourself out of the overwork mentality. *Reduce, reduce, reduce* will become your new mantra, to the tune of about ninety minutes a day. This ninety-minute savings isn't a "guess"—it's what clients have told me these methods have saved them. Take for example the testimonial I received from Montague L. Boyd, CFP, Senior Vice President of Investments at UBS Financial Services:

> Prior to Ms. Stack's training, we customarily had employees who stayed into the early evening hours in order to finish or just keep up with our workload. Ms. Stack spent a day with us and then three or four months later a second day. Ms. Stack worked with us to develop more efficient methods of intra-office communications. Ms. Stack also showed us how to prioritize daily items and to keep track of them. She showed us how to use Microsoft Outlook properly. There are far too many details to recount here; they made a huge difference. Now we regularly find that we can finish our work every day with time to spare. We operate with much less confusion and rarely if ever worry about those items that may "drop through the cracks"! They just don't. There are six investment partners. We have a partner in charge of our Retirement Plan group and a Research partner. We operate smoothly now and communicate effectively in much less time. My estimate is that each of us saves about ninety minutes per day compared to our systems before Laura Stack. Six support staff went from a state of confused, stressed, and long hours to an efficient team. They finish most days well before "quitting time" and go home on time every night. Nobody has stayed late in months. Ms. Stack has lived up to her title as "The Productivity Pro." She has shown us a path to accomplish more—much more—in fewer hours. Our staff believes

they can take us through exponential growth with very little need for additional manpower. All of this extra time gives us the opportunity to think and find other ways to improve our business plan for greater success.

In the same way I helped his team, I will show you how to logically reprioritize your work and shift your focus to the truly significant. You'll learn to jettison old ideas that limit your productivity and begin re-examining your workload with new eyes. You'll excise useless tasks and cut through redundant data to sharpen your focus to a keen edge.

Instead of accepting your fate and allowing it to overwhelm you, step up and take your future in your own hands—and do what's necessary to achieve a work-life balance that you can manage indefinitely. Unlearn the mistaken beliefs that serve as obstacles to productivity. Recognize your limits, trim away the fat, and adjust your attitude until you can plainly see that the *real* issue here is discovering what you can reasonably accomplish within the time available. If you do all this, you'll eventually come to realize that there really *is* time enough in the day to do everything that matters.

With the new system I offer you, it's simple to rearrange your life so you can *have* a life outside of work. Not necessarily easy, mind you—but simple and straightforward to implement. With that in mind, I'd like to introduce the Productivity Workflow Formula™.

A BRAND-NEW MODEL:
THE PRODUCTIVITY WORKFLOW FORMULA™ (PWF)

The PWF breaks down into six primary steps:

1. **Determine what to do.** Study your work requirements closely; triage your to-do lists; handle time-wasters; and decide to do only what really matters.
2. **Schedule time to do it.** Assign time slots and durations

appropriately; say no when appropriate; make decisions quickly; and control your meetings.

3. **Focus your attention.** Hone your concentration to razor sharpness; shut out distractions; learn focus techniques; and avoid multitasking.

4. **Process new information.** Research effectively; file digital information; and quickly handle incoming e-mail, voicemail, and paper.

5. **Close the loop.** Determine what does and doesn't work; reduce inefficiencies; solve people problems and bottlenecks; and tighten up systems as you go.

6. **Manage your capacity.** Focus on the physical factors affecting your energy; manage sleep, diet, exercise, and your own happiness.

Graphically, the PWF looks like this:

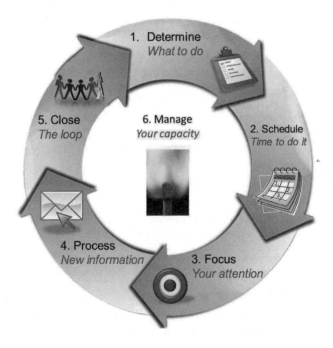

The model is circular by design, which suggests continuity, as well as a process that can (and should) be repeated again and again. In other words, you get into a continuum and don't have to leave it; it just becomes part of your life. Plus, instead of thinking of productivity as a straight line from A to B (followed by . . . nothing) it becomes its own self-fulfilling prophecy. Each improvement gets you to a new place, instead of to some plateau you never leave again.

THE PRODUCTIVITY WORKFLOW FORMULA™ (PWF)
Determine + Schedule + Focus + Process + Close + Manage = PRODUCE

If you incorporate the PWF into your life, you really can save yourself ninety minutes a day that you can use to live your life, instead of working it away. This may sound odd if you feel shackled to your desk now, but it really *is* possible to get more done while doing less work. You just need to separate the valuable wheat from the nonproductive chaff.

So let's take a look at how you can become more efficient, step by logical step.

Go to www.LauraStack.com/WhatToDo to receive complimentary bonus material, tip sheets, and group discussion worksheets.

Go to www.bkconnection.com/whattodo-sa to assess your strengths and improve opportunities around your PWF.

🕐 We've highlighted Productivity Pro tips with a clock icon. If you're seriously pressed for time, skim these tips and read the summary at the end of each chapter.

1

Determine What to Do

The first step in the Productivity Workflow Formula is to determine what you should be working on. When you implement this step correctly, instead of having 117 things on your to-do list, you may end up with just ten tasks, or five, or even three . . . but they'll be the right ones. And don't worry: Once you have the proper processes in place, you can revisit all the others systematically and get them done in their place.

In this chapter, I'll show you how to reduce your commitments to an efficient core group of tasks. In the end, you'll produce for your organization at a record level and work fewer hours than ever before.

Workplace productivity, in its most meaningful sense, is all about achieving high-value goals—preferably in the shortest time possible. And make no mistake about it: At the end of the day, all that truly matters is *results*. What did you actually accomplish? Did your accomplishments advance the organization's goals in some measurable way? If not, why not? If you just kept busy while not appreciably moving forward, why did you bother?

Never confuse activity with productivity. Everyone has too much to do, and nobody really cares how many tasks you crossed off a list or how busy you were last week if key projects keep falling through the cracks.

Therefore, you must pare down your commitments to

include *only* those things that truly matter for you and your organization. Remember: your goal here is to reduce your responsibilities to a reasonable level, so you can go home at a sensible time and have a life outside of work—not try to take on everything, and punish yourself constantly with sixteen-hour days. That will result in plummeting productivity and burnout.

🕐 At the end of every workday, take a moment to ask yourself: Was I productive today, or did I just stay busy?

WHY DO YOU HAVE SO MUCH TO DO?

When you look at your to-do list, does it scare you? Your list is so long, an entire team of people couldn't finish it all. Looking at your huge to-do list, you might feel as though you'll be buried forever and never see the light of day. So before I begin to describe how to reduce your commitments to a reasonable, consistently workable level, let's take a step back and look at the reasons why most of us always seem to have too much to do.

Too many options. There are so many seemingly "good" things to do, and often we want to do as many as we can. The result is a huge running to-do list that doesn't distinguish between today, next week, next month, and next year. Without a separation between the lists, many people stare at a to-do list with hundreds of items on it and have a difficult time choosing what to do when faced with an open thirty minutes.

Bad math. We take inputs without producing outputs. We accept projects, allow interruptions, go to meetings, answer calls, and check e-mail . . . and our to-do list grows longer, but nothing valuable gets checked off.

Pavlovian response. We're slaves to our technology, environment, noises, and brains. We can't overcome inertia, get in the flow, and focus on completing a single task. We respond immediately to every chime, ding, and noise.

Indecision. We don't determine whether tasks are in or out or even relevant or not, so we leave them on our lists, which causes us to have to repeat the evaluation process again—putting them back into our 'decide later' consciousness, lengthening our to-do lists, filling our inboxes, and expanding our perceptions of how much we have to do.

Disorganization. Our tech toys can't keep up with the speed of thought. This is especially inconvenient if you're in a restaurant, meeting, or on a plane with all your electronic devices off, and you think of something to do. We need ways to capture inputs back into the system.

Fear. We can't say no to anything that doesn't meet our stated objectives. We're afraid to take action to cut out the time we waste each day on nonproductive activities.

Lack of direction. We lack clarity from our leadership and haven't taken the time to harness our own focus to determine what really matters. Or we're not aligned with strategy from top to bottom; consequently, we don't have clear priorities. Often, our actual work doesn't reflect our job descriptions or what the boss actually thinks we are/should be doing.

In reality, many of the things on our to-do lists are unnecessary time-stealers. In most cases, they were added because somebody thought it might be a good idea. Watch out for "somebody"; they're not necessarily interested in helping you be productive. In fact, the things they're giving you to do are the things *they* don't want to do. In other words, they feel those tasks aren't worth their time . . . so they decide to steal *your* time instead. To top it off, many of us voluntarily take on tasks that are seemingly unnecessary at first glance (and may actually be), but end up burning time we could otherwise use to be productive.

To get control over your schedule, you must first eliminate anything that doesn't have long-term consequences for your work. Philosopher William James once wrote, "The art of being wise is the art of knowing what to overlook." In other words, in trying to determine what to do, you must first eliminate those tasks that don't enhance your productive value.

WHAT IS YOUR PRODUCTIVE VALUE?

How do you determine your value? Look at what you do from your employer's viewpoint. Simply put, the more productive you are, the more valuable you are to your organization. And let me qualify that by saying where this really matters is *in the long term*. If you shine brightly for a year by working eighty-hour weeks until your body gives up and literally falls over, then your productive value, while extraordinary for a little while, isn't particularly impressive when viewed from a wider perspective. Your organization would rather get ten years of steadily productive work out of you than one extraordinary year before you burn out.

Reducing your commitment load to the bare minimum, so you can most effectively use your time at work (and still enjoy life and recharge for more work), makes you more valuable to the organization. Some bosses lose sight of that sometimes; but most will realize this is in fact the case (especially if you send them a photocopy or scan of this section of the book), and will prefer to keep you rather than lose you permanently . . . one way or another. If you're self-employed, this isn't as much of an issue. But it's still apropos in terms of how it affects your organization, whether you operate a sole proprietorship or an up-and-coming Inc. 500 firm.

So What's Your Personal ROI?

The concept of Personal Return on Investment (PROI) is one that's been steadily gaining currency in the business world over the past few years. While the term can be defined in several ways, in common usage it's just what it sounds like: the investment potential that you, as an employee, offer to your organization. Now, I realize that it may seem somewhat degrading to be treated (and especially to treat yourself) as a mere investment . . . but to some extent, that's precisely what you are: your organization's investment in its human capital.

Like any other resource, you're only as good as your PROI. The harsh realities of survival in the Great Recession have hammered this point home to employers and employees alike. As a modern worker, you've got to be hard-nosed about your ultimate value to your employer. You ignore this at your peril.

Elsewhere in the business world, ROI is defined as the profit realized from a resource minus the original and ongoing investment. It's no different with Personal ROI. In addition to your pay, the organization is probably providing you with various benefits, as well as regular training and/or education, experience in your field, and personal stability. What are you providing in return? The organization is pumping resources and cash into you, so how are you repaying them?

You'd better be returning a substantial multiple of your investment on a consistent basis—and, more important, you have to be able to prove you are. Before you can do that effectively, you'll need to sit down and determine what you bring to the table. Perform a tough, even brutal self-assessment of your value, focusing on these factors:

- What are you really good at?
- What makes you special?
- What distinguishes you from your peers?
- How do you personally help the organization achieve its corporate goals?

As a business resource, your value is dollar-driven. A good rule of thumb is you should be able to prove you've earned or saved the organization at least three times your base salary every single year.

In some jobs, proving your PROI is easy. If you're a salesman who's just landed a $5,000,000 account, it's easy to point to that accomplishment. But not every job directly results in corporate income. For example, what if you work in Human Resources or Customer Service? Well, you'll need to dig deeper for your provable PROI, by showing how deft you are at hiring profitable, productive workers, or maintaining intra-departmental harmony, or soothing the feathers of irate customers—whatever the case may be for your particular position.

If you ever find yourself coming up short, you must be willing to invest your personal capital, especially your time and energy, toward increasing your PROI, so you can thereby make yourself more attractive. In addition to working hard, fast, and smart, don't hesitate to ask for more training or institute new systems to maximize efficiency and performance in your job. These preventive measures are short-term in nature, and they'll pay time-saving (and PROI) dividends for a long time to come.

In calculating your PROI, be reasonably creative about what you've accomplished, and don't leave out anything that might be relevant. Do you have a tendency to finish projects early and under budget? Include that in your assessment, because you've saved the organization money. Are you good with clients, able to develop a positive relationship that lasts for years? Then you've earned the organization money, because that's where profits come from: multiple sales to repeat customers (at a decent margin, of course).

You may not be able to provide a specific dollar amount or percentage for your personal PROI, but you should be able to demonstrate that without you, the organization would be worse off. This is also a great exercise to perform prior to your performance evaluation, so you can have an intelligent conver-

---

🕐 Recalculate your Personal Return on Investment (PROI)
periodically. This will help you determine what
you need to brush up or cut back on.

---

sation with your supervisor about what you've accomplished in
the past period.

And never forget this: You can't assume anyone will automatically realize your worth. So in addition to being able to
prove your PROI when called upon, be proactive about step-
ping forward and demonstrating that hiring you was a positive
investment decision. This is especially true if you feel you're
undervalued, or if some unscrupulous coworker attempts to
take the credit for your work. As the saying goes, the squeaky
wheel gets the grease; but be careful here, because obnoxious
squeakiness can get you the boot instead.

Demonstrate by your actions and initiative that you're
worthy. Then be politely assertive, though not aggressive, in
pointing out your PROI to those who matter in your organization—so you can maximize your value both to the organization and to yourself.

Defining Importance

You may discover that determining what's truly important is
one of your biggest challenges. How do you know if something
you do is important? Sometimes a task's importance isn't immediately obvious. You need some simple guidelines to chan-
nel your efforts.

First, start with your job requirements. Think in terms of
results, not a vague-sounding title or general tasks. What did
the organization really hire you to do? Ask yourself, "Why am
I here?" At the very minimum, what do your superiors expect
you to accomplish on a daily, weekly, monthly, or even an annual basis?

If you made a list of the top ten things you believe you're

responsible for, and then asked your manager to do the same, and compared the two lists, would they be the same? If not, you have a problem, because you aren't spending your time in ways that are valuable to your best customer. Know your manager's requirements cold, both the formal ones on your job description and the informal ones your boss expects you to do anyway. Keep the notes from your last performance review front and center, and make sure you're making progress on them daily.

For example, in a small company such as mine, I'm both the President and Chief Executive Officer (CEO). As the CEO of my organization, I'm responsible for mapping our strategic direction and building our brand. I need to understand trends, conduct research, and write books. As the President, I'm the rainmaker. My job is to give killer keynotes and seminars on strategic platforms, so the referrals and recommendations continue to build the business. This requires me to practice my performances, continuously update my programs, and talk to clients. It's incumbent on me to delegate, hire out, contract, ignore, or eliminate *anything* that doesn't "fit" into one of those buckets. I don't know how to use the fax machine or the postage meter. I *could* use them, of course, but I shouldn't be doing that at my level, so I simply refuse to touch it.

Just because a task is important doesn't mean you're the right person to do it, and even if you are, you still might be doing more work than is necessary. Ask yourself:

- Are you doing things someone else could or should be doing? If so, take steps to rectify the situation.
- Are you working below your pay grade? It's a mistake to waste time on something if someone else can do it more cheaply. Delegate everything you can.
- Are you letting brushfires and crises take up your time? Why? Whose crisis is it?
- Can you cut back on the output of some tasks without others complaining? Do they matter in the end analysis?

🕐 If one of your tasks properly belongs to someone else, hand it back to them—even if they don't want it. Your work must come first, so stop being so darn nice.

Second, determine what's personally important to you: What do you need to do before you leave the office to feel good about what you've accomplished? Be sensible and try to limit yourself to a few core tasks. If you're having trouble determining a task's value, then weigh the consequences of not getting it done. Consider how much each task is really worth, based on the results you achieve and the amount of time you have to spend on it. Who or what would suffer? You? Anyone? If you didn't do it at all, would anyone notice? If you can't figure out why a task needs to be done at all, stop doing it and see what happens. I'm serious. If someone screams, consider putting it back on your list—but only if it's something that affects you in some significant way. As my father (a retired colonel in the U.S. Air Force) used to tell me, "It's easier to ask for forgiveness than to get permission." I tested that one a lot and it generally worked. If I got yelled at, that was a pretty good clue.

For every task, ask, "Who is affected by it, and how?" Remember, you're the most important person in this equation. Is the task a job requirement? Formal or informal? Does it contribute to your immediate objectives? Is it related to your long-term goals? (Do you *have* long-term goals?) Is it necessary to achieve those goals? If the task only benefits someone else without noticeably impacting you in any way, then why are *you* doing it? If possible, hand it off to the person whom it directly affects, and tell them you won't be doing it anymore.

The general idea here is to cut, cut, and cut more. It's best to not have a task on a list in the first place than to continue to think about it, prioritize it, and organize it. Simplify your goals and objectives to a point where you feel good about what you've accomplished each day, week, or month, and your employer feels even better about the results (you've exceeded your PROI).

TRACKING DOWN TIME-WASTERS

Of all the resources available to us, time is certainly the most precious. Unlike office supplies or even money, it's impossible to get more; there's no box marked "Time" in the supply closet where you can grab a spare minute or two. Once time is spent, it's gone, and you can't get it back. And yet, we invariably waste it. Every minute wasted keeps us from doing things we've determined we *should* be doing.

You can't afford to waste time at work. A firm grasp of time management is absolutely crucial if you want to succeed in your workload reduction efforts. When you "manage time," you're ultimately just managing yourself. Where do you need to practice better self-management?

With that in mind, let's take a look at the biggest self-inflicted time-wasters in modern business and how to avoid them.

E-mail. Do you hang out in your inbox all day long? Bad idea! If you drop everything and immediately attend to every e-mail as it comes in, you're derailing your productivity, over and over again. Not only do you waste whatever time it takes for you to read, ignore, or act on a given e-mail message, but you also require more time to refocus your attention on whatever you were doing prior to the interruption.

Let's face it. E-mail can be a phenomenal productivity tool, but it will eat your day alive if you let it. If you simply can't resist looking, then you'll need to shut down your e-mail completely to focus on other tasks. Turn off your alerts as well in your e-mail options, so the tone or the envelope in the system tray won't constantly remind you that there's e-mail waiting.

We'll discuss techniques for handling distractions from e-mail and other technologies in Chapter 3.

The Internet. The Internet has to be the single worst productivity thief in the modern business era. Sure, it's useful, and it can and has built fortunes—but it's also a siren that lures workers onto the rocks of unproductivity. In recent surveys, workers have admitted to wasting an average of two hours per workday, and approximately an hour of it is online.[6] Yikes!

The Internet is a bottomless pit of information . . . some useful and some not-so-useful. It's much too easy to sit down to do one thing (pay a bill or look up an address) and end up wasting time on something else entirely (reading news stories or checking your social networks).

If meandering around the Web is relaxing for you, it's fine when you're ready for a purposeful break. Just make sure you do it at an appropriate time and place, so it doesn't interfere with work time. Otherwise, treat the Internet like any other tool: Use it when you need it, and put it away when you're done.

Social media. Be especially careful with social media sites like Twitter, Facebook, and LinkedIn. From a productivity perspective, they can be time-sucking vampires. I use all three strategically in my business, because they serve a valid marketing purpose for me, as they do for many other entrepreneurs. However, in many jobs and companies, employees aren't using social media to boost annual earnings. To the contrary, they're squandering those earnings. Even those with a valid business reason can waste inordinate amounts of time reading postings and commenting on non-business issues. Think I'm exaggerating? Consider this:

Meet Bob. Bob uses Twitter every day for just twenty minutes during business hours. No big deal, right? Wrong! That comes to one hundred minutes of lost productivity each week. There are fifty-two weeks in a year; let's say Bob gets two

weeks of vacation, so that's five thousand minutes of lost productivity annually, just from Twitter alone. If Bob works for
the organization for ten years, that's fifty thousand minutes of
lost productivity over the course of Bob's career. That works
out to more than 833 hours—twenty-one weeks of lost productivity! And all because Bob is a mild Tweetaholic who Tweets
twenty minutes each day. How has his Tweeting impacted the
bottom line? Now, imagine what happens if you have an organization with five, fifty, five hundred, or five thousand Bobs.

Socializing. We all want a workplace where people get along
and enjoy spending time together. However, too often we're
chatting when we should be working. Chitchat is fine for
lunchtime and breaks, but otherwise you should be working.
You should especially avoid chattering outside someone's office or cubicle, because then you're not just wasting your time,
you're distracting someone else, too. So it's a good idea to set
limits on your social behavior, no matter how much you might
not want to.

Back in 2006, I read with a mixture of interest and amuse-
ment an article referencing a study done by OfficeTeam/
Robert Half International about whether socializing at work
around the water cooler is a waste of time.[7]

Predictably, workers said no. Also predictably, managers
said yes. The answer, of course, is *yes* . . . and *no*. Come now;
this is a silly study. As with any study, it's easy to skew the
numbers. The answers will vary in any case, depending upon
the context of the socializing and your point of reference. You
can't say that all socializing is a waste of time, although some
is, of course. Thirty minutes spent discussing the details of
Aunt Sally's surgery could qualify as a nonproductive activity.
However, some socializing is needed for relationship building,
bonding, camaraderie, and mentoring.

Still, there should come a certain point in the conversation when you realize, "Okay, I've been here long enough
. . . time to move on." That's when you should wrap it up—

immediately, without spending another ten minutes wind-
ing down. If more people would listen to their intuition, we
wouldn't need time-wasting studies such as the one I just cited.

Negativity. Speaking of limits, I can recommend two so-
called "social" activities you should stop altogether: gossiping
and complaining. Not only do they waste time, they're damaging to the corporate culture, which can skewer productivity
even further.

Talking with your buddies should stop short of discussing
other people behind their backs. Airing someone's personal
business for entertainment reasons is never going to help you
achieve anything, and spreading negativity or criticism is
downright hurtful.

As far as complaining goes, we all have things in our lives
we're unhappy about, but grousing about them accomplishes
very little. As for gossiping, all it does is spread negativity,
and who needs more of that? In particular, you should avoid
complaining about the amount of money you make, and how
dissatisfied you may be with your job or coworkers. Instead of
moaning about life, readjust your attitude. If you're disgrun-
tled about things you can't change, learn to accept them, and
move on. If you find yourself complaining about things you *can*
change, then by all means try to.

Handling personal issues. These days, it's too easy for the
rest of your life to intrude on your workday. You can be interrupted by personal messages in myriad ways—IMs, texts,
e-mail, and calls—and you know the remedy. Turn off your
electronics, don't check your personal e-mail, and end any

🕐 We don't like it when people gossip about us, so stop
gossiping about others. It's a hurtful waste of your time.

---

personal calls on the company's phone or your cell phone as quickly as possible.

In addition to communications issues, many of us also allow minor personal business to eat away at our working hours. I've known people to balance their checkbooks, book vacation travel, or sort out their mortgage applications while at work. I suspect people do these things during the workday because they work so many hours . . . by the time they're home . . . it's late and they're exhausted. This is obviously counterproductive. If possible, finish up work on time, leave, and conduct your personal business on your personal time. Some of our globe-trotting schedules don't allow for this nice, neat compartmentalization, but it truly does help with focus to the extent you can make it happen.

Better yet, try to gain flexibility. It's true that life happens, and it isn't always convenient, and some things can only be arranged during the week from 9:00 to 5:00. Fortunately, companies are starting to realize that it's in their best interests to assist employees who are attempting to manage their lives during the day, rather than standing in the way. That can mean anything from allowing workers to access the Internet for incidental personal use to offering flexible schedules to accommodate personal appointments.

If necessary, talk to your boss, your peers, and your staff about finding opportunities for flexibility within the workday. Employees who feel they don't have to accomplish a million things during lunch hour will be more productive during the rest of the day. So do whatever you can to promote a reasonable work-life balance—but realize there's only so far you can go in the "life" direction without damaging workplace productivity. Once you hit that limit, you'll need to leave your personal business at home. Then go home and leave work at work. There's always a blurring of boundaries you can't avoid, especially when you own a company, but it does make sense to draw boxes around each one as much as possible.

Smoking. I'm sure I'll get e-mails on this, but some workers have a ready-made excuse for wasting time: they're smokers. Of course, it is your choice to smoke; however, you should only do so on regularly scheduled breaks or at lunch, within the parameters your employer has set. Not all smokers follow the rules, because they need more cigarettes than the rules allow. Many smokers often take extra time here and there to nurse their addiction. Given the fact that most employers don't make this easy anymore, it can take ten minutes or more to get to the designated smoking area, smoke a cigarette, and get back to work. That can add up to a lot of wasted time per workday. The solution? Kick the habit.

Arriving late/leaving early. This one's self-explanatory. Many of us pare a few minutes off the day occasionally, and some of us make a habit of it. It may not seem like much, but get this: if you're late or leave early an average of just ten minutes a day, that adds up to about a week's paid vacation over the course of a year. Better start setting that alarm earlier.

Boring or unpleasant tasks. It's difficult to get motivated to complete mundane tasks. You'll focus much better on your important work if you don't have all those less-interesting tasks hanging over your head. So jump in and get them done! About 99 percent of the time, those nitpicky tasks are dramatically easier and less painful than you expect. Getting started is the hardest part. If you're really having trouble, schedule a five-minute appointment with yourself to begin the chore. When the designated time arrives, start working on the task. If you feel like stopping at the end of five minutes, you can. The only rule is, you must schedule an additional five minutes for tomorrow. When you begin to see some progress, five minutes soon becomes ten, fifteen, and then twenty. Sometimes you just need some momentum.

WHERE DOES YOUR TIME GO?

The solution to all these time-wasters is simple enough: "Stop!" However, what if you're not even sure where all your time is going? Paralysis can derail your efforts to reduce your commitment load and prioritize what remains. If so, spend a week logging how you spend your time during the week, activity by activity. Include everything, not just your important tasks. You can get a complimentary copy of a time-log worksheet, instructions, and debriefing guide on my website.[8]

With your logs in hand, ask yourself these questions:

- How aligned is my time use with my top priorities?
- What should I stop doing?
- What do I need to do more of?
- What am I not doing that I need to do?

To further clarify your time-use situation, you can adopt the approach Michael Bungay Stanier outlines in his book *Do More Great Work*. Separate what you have on your plate into BAD work (mind-numbing, non–value-adding tasks), GOOD work (largely what your employer expects from you) and GREAT work (important work that feeds your soul, and will make a huge difference if only you can find the time to do it). The goal, of course, is to reduce or eliminate Bad work and to address Good work—for example, by delegating it to someone who would consider it their Great work—so as to find more time and energy for *your* Great work. Michael's book provides fifteen maps to help you sort it all out and get moving.[9]

Stay On Point

As you know, you can't really manage time (or else you'd be able to do a really good job and create a thirty-hour day, instead of a twenty-four-hour day). You can really manage only yourself, so make a sincere effort to protect your limited stockpile of minutes—not just from others, but from yourself. Stop trying to do everything!

There *will* be enough time to do the most important things if you're efficient about it. So make your time-saving decisions authoritatively, and move forward without worrying. Remember, even if you work for someone else, the buck ultimately stops with you. *You* are in control of what you accomplish each day. When you take charge this way, you can focus on the truly important—and stop wasting time on things that don't matter in the long run.

If you identify one or more of these time-wasters in your daily routine, here's my recommendation: Choose the worst one, determine how to fix it, and discipline yourself to put what you've learned into play. Once you have a handle on that time-waster, move to another. I think you'll be surprised at how much productive time you'll free up over the long run.

Create a *Not*-To-Do List

One of my absolute favorite quotes, which I like so much it's in my e-mail signature, is by the late, great Peter Drucker, who once pointed out, "There is nothing so useless as doing efficiently that which should not be done at all."

As a result of the analysis you've done so far in this chapter, it would be a great idea to compile a *Not*-To-Do list—a list of things you simply refuse to do. This type of list is central to my unifying theme of reducing your commitment load and teasing that extra ninety minutes out of your work schedule.

A not-to-do list need not be fancy. Just start by writing down the time-wasting behaviors you should avoid. Then include the misaligned tasks that end up on your plate because you're "being nice." Then review and revise your list periodi-

⊕ Prepare a list of time-wasting things you refuse to do. Keep this *Not*-To-Do list close, and refer to it frequently.

cally, to make sure you don't accidentally slip into habits that damage your productivity and keep you at work too long. For example:

- Don't do low-profit or low-priority work when you can delegate it instead.
- Don't let brushfires and crises suck up all your time.
- Don't spend all your time at work at the expense of family and friends.
- Don't deal with work issues during personal time—and vice-versa.
- Don't procrastinate.
- Don't fall prey to perfectionism.
- Don't attend useless meetings.
- Don't gossip or complain.
- Don't multitask.
- Don't let your electronics hamper rather than help you.
- Don't waste work time on social sites or the Internet.
- Don't check your e-mail more than a few times per day, unless your job requires it.
- Don't check your morals and values at the door.
- Don't undervalue those you work with.
- Don't wait until the last minute to do important things.
- Don't micromanage.

This sample list only scratches the surface; but you get the point. Obviously, not-to-do lists will vary from person to person, based on what applies to a particular workplace and what each individual considers impractical or illogical. Decide you'll only tackle tasks that are necessary, and don't waste your time on things that shouldn't be done. Scaling back and eliminating tasks and time-wasters from your life might seem counterintuitive, insofar as productivity is concerned. You might think the key to productivity is getting more done each day. This is far from true. You don't need a calendar full of unnecessary tasks to be productive and accomplish more.

Conscious thought is the first key to learning to scale back your daily commitments, so you can take back time that you ought to spend on the rest of your life. Study your obligations and work requirements closely so you can determine what's necessary and what isn't.

TO-DO LISTS: TRACKING WHAT'S LEFT

Everything you haven't eliminated thus far has to be tracked and organized. Many people assume because there's a crumpled up to-do list on the cover of this book, I'm against to-do lists. Not true! The paper wad is symbolic of the frustration people feel when they look at a single, giant, overwhelming list.

You do need to-do lists to stay organized; in this section, we'll discuss not just one, but two lists. (There are other types of lists, which we'll discuss later so as not to confuse the issue.)

1. A limited daily to-do list, which I call a HIT list, since it contains all the High Impact Tasks (HITs) that keep your workflow humming along.

2. A Master list, which contains all future projects and tasks, "someday" items, and good ideas you're not yet ready to work on.

You must separate what you need to do today from what you don't need to do today. Combining the two is very distracting and makes it difficult to determine what to work on next. Let's review these two lists in detail.

🕐 Instead of putting all your tasks on one huge list,
establish separate HIT (daily) and master lists
so you can prioritize appropriately.

The Daily HIT List

Your HIT list includes a reasonable number of items that you honestly plan to accomplish on a particular day. Most of your day-to-day activities will consist of tasks funneled to you during meetings, e-mails, phone calls, and verbal communication. (We'll discuss how to process incoming information into these lists in Chapter 4.)

The HIT list isn't a repository for *everything* you want to accomplish. By design, a daily HIT list literally guides your day's work, so be realistic when compiling it. If you have three hours of meetings, and you know you'll have a bunch of e-mail, and you know you'll be interrupted by coworkers, clients, and your boss—and you need to take bio breaks—why would you plan seventeen hours of work for yourself? If your daily HIT list contains more than ten items, I'd say you're stretching it.

HIT list items might include these tasks:

- Send agreement to XYZ client.
- Work on PowerPoint deck.
- Finalize monthly earnings report.
- E-mail Johnny's teacher about running club.
- Conduct statistical analysis of marketing results.
- Write article for company newsletter.
- Call CSU College of Business to schedule tour.

If used properly, your HIT list can be one of your most powerful productivity tools. It's a great way to manage up as well. It's important to ask, "Which is more important—this XYZ task I'm working on currently or this task you just put on my plate? If I handle this new task, I may not be able to finish this other one today as promised." When my office manager Becca has done this with me, I have removed things from her plate instantly.

The Master List

The Master list is a running list of *everything* you need or want to do at some point. (This is what some people have been using as a daily to-do list until now.) While items on the HIT list may rank as important in the short term, you can't allow them to overwhelm the long-term projects and tasks needed to achieve true workplace success. Whenever something important comes in that lacks urgency or has no set deadline, add it to the Master list, so you have a running compilation of all the things you want to do eventually but don't need to do today.

Many of the strategic goals of your company, department, and team will end up here, along with "someday" ideas like revamping old workflow systems and inventing new ones, or your intention to learn a new language. Your Master list keeps your daily HIT list from overflowing into uselessness, and may consist of dozens or hundreds of entries as a result.

Master list items might include:

- Hire a new assistant.
- Research new customer relationship management (CRM) software.
- Download barcode app.
- Buy new printer.
- Create QR code for business card.
- Find WordPress plug-in for membership sites.
- Get landscaping estimates for backyard.

A Master list should be a perpetual work in progress: a living, evolving document guiding long-term workflow. You

---

🕑 Perform a "brain-dump" of all your important but nonurgent tasks, as well as all the "someday" tasks you want to accomplish. This will form the basis of your master to-do list.

---

can't let it turn into a dead file for forgotten tasks. To keep it at the top of your mind, your Master list has to flow into your HIT list, so that each day, you're not only doing the urgent, but you're working on the important as well.

The Flow from Master to HIT

Every time you think of something you need to do, ask yourself, "Is this something I need to do TODAY?" If yes, put it on your HIT list. If no, add it to your Master list.

We'll talk through many different organizing options in Chapter 4, but in general, if you're using a paper planner, write the task on the appropriate daily page for the HIT list. The Master list would be a separate paper list you file behind a tabbed section or the "M" tab for "Master."

Personally, I like using Outlook Tasks for my Master list, because the Master list automatically becomes the HIT list, without having to think about it. To set it up:

- Change the "Arrange By" field in your To-Do Bar to Start Date (not the default "Due Date"—why would you want to know something is due today if it will take three days to work on it?).
- When you think of something to do, fill in the Start Date on the day you need to begin that activity or want to think about it again. Enter the Due Date for the day it's due. (If you fill in only the "Due Date" field, you will see that item on your Task Pad every day.)
- Name your Categories with your key projects. Brainstorm a list of all Tasks needed to complete each project and assign Start and Due dates for each piece. Tag each Task with the correct Category, so you can view your Tasks "By Category" to see a list of all Tasks related to a particular project.
- The "Today" flag in the To-Do bar now becomes your HIT list, since Tasks move themselves forward automatically.

- Leave the Start and Due Dates blank for "someday" items, so they appear under the "No Date" flag and can be reviewed systematically.

The Review Process

Once you make your lists, you should conduct three reviews of them:

1. *Monthly Forward Thinking.* Review your calendar and project plans to determine what you need to complete by the end of the month. Assign Start Dates for those "someday" items ready to move into your daily consciousness. What deadlines are approaching, what project steps should be started, what meetings do you need to prepare for, what travel arrangements do you need to make, and so on. Delete out-of-date items or those that will never happen for one reason or another.

2. *Weekly Reverse Thinking.* Review the past week's daily pages for incomplete activities and missed items. Where did you leave a message and didn't get a return call? Where did someone cancel an appointment that you need to reschedule? What didn't get done that needs to? When did you forget to send a thank-you present to a client? Make sure you move any follow-up to the appropriate day for action. The most successful performers are not only self-starters; they are self-finishers as well.

3. *Evening Daily HIT List Triage.* Let's say you end up with ten tasks on your HIT list. The average HIT list will contain a mix of items with different priorities, originating from a variety of sources. By necessity, urgent but relatively unimportant items will dominate your list. But you must also

---

🕑 Triage your master list occasionally to cull any tasks you will clearly never do, or those that are out of date.

work in the non-urgent but essential tasks—that is, the things that count most in the long run. So when you're faced with a block of discretionary time, what should you do first? Before you leave work each day, order your tasks for the following day using the triage system below. If an unexpected task pops up, triage it accordingly and work it into the list.

🕐 Before closing down shop for the day, spend 15 minutes reviewing the tasks on your HIT list for the next day. Determine priorities, so you know in what order to tackle them.

TRIAGE: WARTIME PRIORITIZATION

Many of us fall into the trap of considering a HIT list a "Must Do" list, even if doing so requires a sixteen-hour day. You do *not* have to complete everything on it before leaving the office. If a task has relatively minimal significance, or you just don't have time for it, then let it go—at least temporarily. Don't assume everything is sacred; that just leads to overwork and all the negative things that come with it. Given life's unpredictability, flexibility is a must.

How do you practice flexibility? Decide in advance which of your planned tasks you can drop at a minute's notice, if necessary. To cut your commitment load to a bearable level—and thus recapture that daily ninety minutes or more that you deserve—the concept of triage is crucial.

The term 'triage' derives from the medical field, where it's applied to the need to assign levels of care based on degrees of patient urgency. It literally means, "The sorting out and classification of patients or casualties to determine priority of need and proper place of treatment."

In a hospital emergency room, a triage nurse decides which patients need to be seen immediately and which ones can wait for care, based on the relative severity of their conditions. The concept of first-come, first-served goes right out the window, as well it should; priority becomes paramount. Triage exists so the doctor's time isn't spent taking care of someone who has the flu, while another patient is bleeding to death all over the emergency room floor.

HIT list triage may not be as momentous as its medical namesake, but it does act as a form of preventive medicine for your productivity. Just as the triage nurse has to decide which patients need the most attention, you must determine which tasks on your list take priority over the rest. Those are the ones to focus on; everything else is secondary, to be taken care of only when the top-priority tasks are completed.

In wartime situations, due to the high number of casualties, time is of the essence. Accordingly, medical personnel have adopted assessment systems to shorten the task of prioritization. Most NATO armies use a procedure to divide the wounded into four groups by priority (P):[10]

- P1: Not breathing (life or death)
- P2: Bleeding (can become a crisis as time passes)
- P3: Broken bones (can become problematic if left untreated)
- P4: Burns (painful, requires long-term reconstruction)

They may adjust as necessary, depending upon the severity of the injury. P1 items require immediate attention (if you lose a heartbeat, you're done). The other categories are more flexible. A wounded soldier might have extensive burns that are more serious than someone with a small wound with little blood loss. Such a soldier might require P2 treatment rather than P4, so the label is more important than the examples.

🕐 Stop viewing your HIT List as a "Must Do" list. Instead, consider it a "Want to Do" list, and stay flexible.

Consider your current HIT list. What are the equivalents?

- P1: You will get fired if this isn't done today.
- P2: A valuable long-term activity that should be done soon (often from the Master list).
- P3: Someone will be unhappy if you don't do this eventually.
- P4: Human "pain-management" activities such as socializing and Facebook.

What *must* you accomplish today? If you have a meeting in an hour and haven't finished preparing your presentation, this is obviously critically important, and should be taken care of right away (P1). Your strategic plan may need an update, requiring a few hours of focused thought (P2). On the other hand, if you need to return a call to a vendor, it's much less important, even though the person makes a return call *seem* urgent (P3). As a percentage, most incoming e-mail is unimportant (P3), but if you don't check it for two days, your boss might be unhappy (P1). You can even eliminate some tasks from your list of priorities. Cleaning out the break-room refrigerator might not be a task you should ever tackle (P4), no matter how much you have the urge.

Remember that everyone's priorities are different. It's up to you to determine the priority of each task on your to-do list. As you evaluate each entry, think about the hospital emergency room and ask yourself, "Is this task life or death?" This will help you to determine what needs to be handled at once (P1), what needs to be taken care of later in the day or perhaps the next few days (P2), what can wait even a few weeks if necessary (P3), and what can be eliminated or shouldn't be done (P4). When you know the relative importance of each task, you can find an appropriate time to tackle it.

Remember to be a bit flexible. There are the urgent P1 and P2 tasks you need to tend to ASAP; as such, they represent the bread and butter of your HIT list. However, you should also leave space on your daily list for less pressing P2 and P3 items from your Master list. Often, these items have no particular urgency, so you must be proactive and work on them a bit at a time rather than allow them to languish and become crises.

As your day progresses, new emergencies might come up, and these need to be added to your schedule. The emergency room would never turn away a dying patient simply because they weren't on the schedule in the morning.

Meanwhile, work toward eliminating those tasks that are unnecessary. This might be the equivalent of someone coming into the emergency room with the sniffles or a paper cut. These tasks don't matter and shouldn't be cluttering up your schedule. People aren't going to get upset with you for not doing the things that don't matter. Purely reactive busyness will get you nowhere; your work must be underlain and supported by the solid bedrock of job requirements, strategic goals, process maintenance, and other important but non-urgent items.

Constantly analyze your lists to determine where you can scale back. Triage ruthlessly and change your priorities when you must. By doing so, you'll find you can cut out many tasks altogether. Do what you should do without venturing into not-to-do territory. The time you save will help you work toward that extra ninety minutes a day. This is one portion of the extra time you'll gain to recharge, reconnect with life and family, and prepare for upcoming challenges.

SUMMARY: PWF STEP 1 CHECKUP

You can't exorcise the demon of overwork until you first determine exactly which tasks you need to perform on a regular basis, and then commit to doing only those tasks whenever possible. Start by studying your work requirements closely, and then make a sincere effort to apply the medical concept of triage to your task lists. Cut back or eliminate the time-wasters and set out to do only what truly matters. Common offenders include:

- Paying too much attention to e-mail
- Overuse of the Internet, including social networks
- Excess socializing
- Handling personal issues on the clock
- Smoking
- Arriving late/leaving early
- Too many meetings

Many of our reasons for having too much to do are hollow, with tasks imposed on us by other people, or taken on because of bad math, indecision, disorganization, fear, or lack of direction. Cut back on tasks that have no long-term consequences for your job, so you can catch enough breath to recover from work and enjoy the rest of your life. The concept of triage really comes into its own here, because it helps you establish task priorities on the fly, and push aside anything minor either until you can take care of it, or until it drops off your to-do list.

Speaking of to-do lists, don't just toss everything willy-nilly onto one big list and then expect to be anything but overwhelmed. Leverage the concept of the Master list, where you put all fundamental and "someday" tasks—the important but non-urgent items—while funneling the "right now" tasks to your daily HIT list, where you can handle them right away. Furthermore, compile a *Not*-To-Do list, where you track the things you refuse to clog your schedule with.

The more you can trim the waste out of your schedule, the more valuable you become to your organization—because you're much more productive than before, even though you may work fewer hours. Too many people confuse activity with productivity, forgetting that staying busy doesn't necessarily mean creating results, no matter how many hours you work.

If you just shift your focus to the right things, you can do more in eight hours than you did in twelve before—and you'll preserve your health and sanity along the way.

2

Schedule Time to Do It

In the first step of the Productivity Workflow Formula, we worked on reducing your to-do lists. After you've eliminated time-wasting behaviors and determined exactly what you should do each day, the second step is finding the time to do it—literally—on your calendar. This will require you to structure your schedule very carefully to ensure maximum productivity. Among other things, schedule your tasks effectively, say no when appropriate, and control your meetings—whatever's necessary to efficiently use your time.

After all, time isn't like money, office supplies, or Brussels sprouts. We've each got a very limited amount of it, and we're not going to get any more. In fact, what we call time management isn't "time" management at all. Since everyone has precisely the same amount of time (lacking that spiffy little device Hermione Granger used in the Harry Potter books to take more than one class at once), time management is better regarded as *self*-management. Your management of time is based largely on your willingness to stop *misusing* time—thereby eliminating those things hindering your productivity and protecting your time from those who want a piece of it.

Let's look at a few ways you can further tighten up your time-use habits by creating *new* behaviors to complete your important tasks.

ABOUT THAT 4-HOUR WORKWEEK IDEA

Back in 2007, Timothy Ferriss created a sensation in the business world with his provocatively titled book *The 4-Hour Workweek*. In it, he outlined his philosophy, which I'll paraphrase: Once you've worked hard to build your business, it's possible to maintain it at a profitable level by working just a few hours per week.

Ferriss believes the rules that bind us to the 9-to-5 grind are a pointless legacy of a time long past, because in the modern knowledge economy, what matters isn't how many hours you work—it's how well you perform. Furthermore, he asserts, it doesn't matter how much money you make if you don't have the time to enjoy it.

Using his personal example, Ferriss outlines a method of ruthless time management using (among other things) the 80/20 principle, extreme outsourcing, and what he calls "cultivating selective ignorance"—that is, *not* trying to constantly keep up with every little thing at all times. Instead, he suggests, just catch up whenever it's necessary to do so. This allows you to narrow your focus to the critical few items that really matter, so you can cut your workweek to a length that seems ridiculously short to many of us.

All this seems to work for Tim Ferriss— but can it work for you? Is a 4-Hour Workweek *really* possible? The answer is . . . well, kinda.

I'm with Ferriss on the basics. I've founded my entire business on teaching people how to cut out the extraneous and develop better time-management skills to boost efficiency. I agree wholeheartedly that it's an excellent idea to delegate and/or outsource everything except the few tasks that are the most profitable and valuable to you. As you'll see at some length in the next chapter, I'm all for the process of selective ignorance (i.e., eliminating distractions and interruptions).

Certainly, all these things can help you decrease your work load, especially when you apply them as rigorously as Ferriss apparently does. But does he *really* have a 4-Hour Workweek? I doubt it. First of all, the title of his book is clearly a catchy exaggeration, intended to drive sales. And Ferriss appears, in fact, to work much more than four hours a week, not just in promoting his books, but in maintaining his business interests and a blog.

But however long his workweek is, Ferriss's construct works for him because he has redefined the concept of work. In the context of the 4-Hour Workweek, work is *anything you don't like doing*. Sounds like a great excuse for workaholism, because this definition means anything productive and profitable you enjoy doesn't count as work—no matter how long or hard you work at it. Some observers consider this specious reasoning; to them, work is work, even when it's fun—because no matter what, it takes time, effort, and focus. Others point out that if you're not your own boss, this concept doesn't really apply; you have to fulfill the requirements of your job description, like it or not.

I can see their points, but I can see Ferriss's as well. In fact, one lesson I think we can take away from *The 4-Hour Workweek* is this: if you truly want to maximize your productivity, you have to enjoy what you do. So yes, go ahead and use his methods (and others) to pare your work life down to its essentials, the critical few things all of us time-management gurus tell you to focus on. Then look at them critically; if you don't love them already, *learn* to love them—or change careers. There's nothing as soul-crushing as grinding your way through a job you don't like.

The concept of the 4-Hour Workweek is a valuable one, but, like so many other business concepts, it only works under specific conditions. Ferriss had already built his existing business to steady profitability before he was able to abandon his eighty-hour workweeks for so-called four-hour ones. So this is a maintenance concept; if you're an entrepreneur who's still building your business, don't expect to work four hours a week. Of course, if you work for someone else, don't expect them to

🕐 If you don't already, learn to love what you do
—or change careers. You can't maximize your
productivity if you don't enjoy your work.

respond well to the concept (that sentence actually made me laugh aloud while writing).

Moreover, this method can't possibly work for every business, no matter how well-established. The concept of "fun work isn't really work" aside, you can pare down work only so far in a business requiring your constant presence—especially a service business where *you* are the product. For instance, musicians must be present at their gigs every night, so there's only so much they can delegate. A speaker like me is paid to be on the platform. The turning point of a business like this, of course, comes when you're so much in demand you can charge whatever you like for your services. Then you can scale back to the number of hours that suits you.

Much of it depends upon your ability to get good help. Delegating and outsourcing your mundane or administrative tasks sounds good, but let's face it: good help is hard to find. Finding a customer-service person who can get a transaction right is hard enough; finding someone you depend on to run critical functions in your organization is even harder.

SCHEDULING 101

Ultimately, the idea of the 4-Hour Workweek is somewhat misleading, but the basic concepts underlying it are sound. You may never cut your workweek back to just four hours by following it, especially if you're someone else's employee, but you can certainly trim a lot of unnecessary fat from your schedule. Bottom line, you know you must fully commit to making the changes necessary to take control of your time.

Follow Basic Scheduling Principles

Delegate or outsource whenever possible. Get rid of the tasks other people can do more cheaply and more effectively than you can. Get over the idea that if you want something done right, you have to do it yourself; this could be one of the reasons you're stuck in your office all the time. Trust your direct reports to do their jobs, until they prove they can't; don't hover over them or waste time nitpicking their work. If you can delegate without micromanaging, you'll be able to recapture a significant portion of your lost time.

Create your own deadlines. If someone hands you a casual project with no official deadline, set one for yourself. Determine how long the full project will take. Then calculate how many days and how much time you'll need to complete it by your deadline by planning backward. If necessary, schedule personal milestones—that is, self-imposed intermediate deadlines—and break large tasks into segments. They'll help you stay on track and keep an eye on the big picture, especially if the final deadline is far in the future.

Set priorities but be flexible. Construct your HIT and Master lists based on the value-weighted priorities you define. Try to maintain these priorities once you have them sorted, but realize you'll have to reprioritize on the fly occasionally. For example, if you fall behind on a deadline, you may have to schedule extra time for that task on a particular day, and/or reprioritize the task to earlier in the day. Allow a little flexibility into your calendar, so you can productively deal with

⊕ If someone hands you a project without a deadline,
set one yourself to help you stay on track.

crises and other unexpected events—but not too much! If you use up that time on a particular day, fine; if not, then you can leave the office on time.

Take the time of day into account. Think about the time of day you should work on certain tasks to get them done most efficiently and effectively, based on your personal biological cycles. Most productivity experts tell you to tackle the most critical and difficult tasks early in the day, and I have no beef with that if you're a "morning person." However, I also think you should save some of these tasks for the time of day when you have the most energy. For most of us, this is during the morning hours; but for others, the peak energy period occurs before or after lunch or even in the evening. You're the expert on *you*, so keep track of your daily peak energy period, and hammer on some of your tough tasks during those periods, when your brain functions better. Leave simpler tasks for low-energy, "secondary time."

🕐 Practice purposeful abandonment, letting low-priority tasks drop off your list—at least temporarily.

Establish Routines

Many athletes have intricate routines for every little thing, such as a free throw in basketball (how many times to dribble the ball, timing, positioning, type of motion, and so on). Once they've fine-tuned everything to their satisfaction, they no longer have to think about the perfunctory portion of their game, and simply execute against it. Albert Einstein took routines to an extreme. For example, he had five identical suits in his closet, so he didn't have to waste mental energy deciding what he was going to wear each day. He just grabbed a clean suit.

I don't mean to undervalue spontaneity, as there's a time

🕐 Establish daily routines for common work tasks, such as checking e-mail or organizing your day. This allows you to make fewer decisions, reducing your energy expenditure.

and a place for it, but without a routine, other people will happily dictate your day for you. In other words, if you don't determine what you need to accomplish and schedule the time to do it, other people are going to be perfectly happy to fill up your day for you.

Apply the idea of routines to all areas of your life, for anything you do on an ongoing basis. Routines help in so many ways:

- They reduce energy expenditure. You won't have to make so many decisions.
- They reduce anxiety. You'll have a plan in place for how to fulfill each activity.
- They build anticipation. Just as setting up a vacation in advance helps build excitement, defined routines can build anticipation . . . and sometimes motivate you when you're slogging through a dull task, if the fun time is already scheduled!

Here are a few helpful ways I've introduced routines into my life:

- Every weekend I'm in town, I have a scheduled date night every Saturday night with my husband.
- Every morning I'm in town, my husband and I go to the recreation center to work out at 7:00 A.M. Period. No excuses.
- I have a monthly "fun day" for a pedicure, manicure, and a massage.
- At the end of each day, I plan the next day.

- Our morning and evening routines with the children create structure and predictability, while minimizing hassle.
- From 10:00 to 11:30 A.M.—when I'm at my highest level of energy—I work on my most creative, difficult tasks.

Routines allow you to build time for reality into your schedule. Block out the time for the report you have to write. If someone tells you a meeting is going to take two hours, block out at least that long. If part of your job is to supervise the work of others in your team, make sure you give yourself time to do so. Make a reasonable estimate of the required time to complete routine tasks and block out the time to do them.

Structure Your Workday Properly

I'm the 2011–2012 president of the National Speakers Association (NSA), and often meet fascinating people at our meetings. One such person was Rick Searfoss, a former astronaut, who brings the lessons of teamwork, leadership, innovation, and peak performance he learned in human spaceflight down to earth for all to enjoy. I asked him what he'd learned about time management by being an astronaut, and if there was such a thing as productivity in outer space.

Rick told me there are certain activities when blasting off that are timed literally down to the second, such as the precise time to ignite the engines. But not all activities are timed, such as housekeeping, eating, restroom breaks, and so on. The astronauts struck a balance between having structure and having flexibility. They planned for the important things, allowing some movement on the lower-priority tasks.

So how does that apply to the real-life work situations we non-astronauts face? Basically, the lesson here is to make sure you block out time to get all the important things done first, and then allow some leeway with your secondary priorities. With that in mind, grab your calendar and start plugging tasks into time blocks. You should plug every top-priority task from your HIT lists into your schedule if possible. It doesn't matter if it's a big task or a small one; estimate how long it will take to do, then block out the time. Yes, actually put an appointment on your calendar and mark it as "busy." No one needs to know you're the only one invited to the meeting.

Basic Scheduling Categories

You can break down the process of scheduling into three steps. Fill in the:

1. Non-negotiable items.
2. Regular daily tasks.
3. Work from your HIT list.

Non-negotiable items are integral to your organization's operations. Let's say your boss schedules a staff meeting every Wednesday morning at 9:00. That's a have-to. If you're in the hospital, on the operating table, you could probably get out of the meeting; if not, forget it. Perhaps you have an ops briefing at 7:30 A.M. You may also have to fill out the weekly time sheet that accounting uses to charge your time to various projects every Friday before you leave. Your son needs his allergy shot Mondays at 4:00, and so on. You rarely have control over have-to tasks, so you might as well plug them in so you can work around them.

Next, plug in your regular daily tasks. This includes things like any statistical or data tracking you're required to do as part of your job, time you block off for client calls, and checking on the status in your area of responsibility. These tasks are a regular and necessary part of your routine. If they aren't, then why are you doing them? If a regular task isn't helping the organization fulfill its goals, get rid of it. If you have to let something slide, you could ignore this appointment in a pinch.

What's that? You'd *like* to get rid of it, but your boss makes you do it? Well, have you written any sort of document to present to your boss, explaining what the task actually costs, and

🕐 Once you've filled your schedule, stop.
You'll always have more tasks than time.

how little return the organization is getting for the cost? Have you tried to convince her that the organization is wasting money by having you do it? If not, why not? Even if your boss assigned you the task, proving it isn't in the best interest of the organization is the best way to get her to change her mind.

Now that you've gotten the have-to and regular daily tasks on the schedule, it's time to start on your to-do list items. Keep in mind the relative priorities of the tasks you've decided to include on your HIT list, and stay focused on the few high-priority tasks (P1 and P2). Don't put *everything* in your calendar and attempt to plan your entire day to the minute, or it will blow up within the first five minutes. But do schedule the most important tasks, especially if one requires a larger block of time. Find a balance between importance and size of the task when trying to fill in your schedule. Leave open some time for interruptions and e-mail (more on this later).

I can almost guarantee you'll get to the end of the time available on your schedule before you get to the end of your HIT list. So, what are you going to do with the rest of the stuff on the list? Triage it and reduce, reduce, reduce! Otherwise, you'll never recapture that extra ninety minutes a day that you need to help you recharge for tomorrow's tasks. Don't make the common mistake of shortening your estimate for some tasks, so you can squeeze a few more in. Cutting the amount of time you allocate to a task won't get it done any faster.

Similarly, adding extra tasks to your schedule won't ensure they'll get done. There's always more work than there is time to do it. So, you've got to determine what you're able to do, what piece of the project you're going to complete, and then STOP! You've already plugged the most important stuff into your schedule. Everything else is just going to have to wait until tomorrow or next week.

Remember those secondary tasks you cut during the triage process? They should drop off the list, because in reality, even if you put them in your schedule, that's what's going to happen. So be honest with yourself and recognize that some tasks won't get done, and just take them off your HIT list. Remember, you're trying to reduce your commitment load so you can produce more. That's your primary goal. At the end of the week, you'll say, "I got this done"—unlike most people, who can only say, "I worked lots of hours."

FURTHER REDUCING YOUR COMMITMENTS

Even within the constraints of your established schedule, you can still influence the length of time you have to spend on each task—particularly if you apply creativity, honesty, and assertiveness to hold on to your time and keep things from ballooning out of control. Let's look at two simple ways you can do it.

How Long Will This Take?

Many times, all it takes to trim a task down to size is to ask the question, "How long will this take?" You should ask yourself and others this question every time a task crosses your path. Consider, for example, how this might work with meetings. When you ask that question, you make the person scheduling the meeting responsible for completing it within a certain time period. If it doesn't finish on time, you can always excuse yourself, saying you put something else on your agenda based on the stated end time. Remind other attendees in advance of your commitment when the meeting begins.

Be willing to leave a meeting if it doesn't finish on time or wanders into uncharted territory.

The Caching Concept

You can also take a cue from the computer field and use the concept of "caching" to improve your productivity. A computer stores the data you've used most recently in its active memory, because you're likely to need that data again and will want to access it quickly. If it can grab the data from the cache, it won't need to go to the extra trouble (and time) of finding the data elsewhere. In short, a good cache improves your computer's performance.

To be time-effective, a computer cache must meet three criteria:

1. It must contain the data you need most of the time.
2. It can never be either completely empty or completely full.
3. It must regularly delete unused data while adding fresh, useful data.

You can also apply this concept to personal availability. "Availability caching" is most critical when you find yourself at or near maximum capacity. While you can't calculate decisions as fast as a computer, you *are* the programmer of your workload. If you can learn to add, drop, and refuse new "data" on the fly, it becomes much easier to streamline your workflow and achieve that extra ninety minutes or so per day you need to retain your health and sanity. Your decisions about to whom to give your time become more automatic, objective, and logical—and ideally, other people will find them easier to appreciate.

🕐 Hold onto your time with both hands. Don't let anyone (even your boss) easily take it away from you by adding items to your task lists without a discussion.

LEARN TO SAY NO—AND MAKE IT STICK

If you really want to limit your availability and put fences around your time, you'll have to shackle the worst time bandit there is: yourself. Most of us are simply too generous with our time—and when you're trying to reach peak productivity, you can't always give in when someone tries to lay claim to your attention—or you'll fill your cache with no room for additions.

So let me remind you of a very important word: "No." I expect it was one of the first words you learned as a child. It's a really easy word to say . . . and a hard one to use. The trick is learning *when* to say it, and realizing it should enjoy a prominent place in your vocabulary.

Why Is It So Hard to Say No?

Unless you're blunt by nature, you may find it difficult to turn people down. Perhaps your parents taught you to be polite to everyone or to respect authority; I can certainly understand that conundrum. But if this is the case, you'll constantly have to guard against people trying to take advantage of your good nature—because believe me, they *will* try.

Or perhaps your work environment is more cutthroat and confusing than most of us like. For example, perhaps you're afraid someone will come back with an aggressive "Why not?" when you say no. The fear of being on the spot and trying to justify yourself may cause you to hesitate. Or you may not want to say no because you're afraid of hurting another person's feelings. If so, why are you taking the other person's feelings into account and not your own?

Similarly, some of us are hesitant to say no because we fear being labeled as having a bad attitude or not being a team player. This is an understandable fear, especially if the person trying to capture some of your time is an authority figure. You may also encounter this problem if you work in an especially competitive environment, where not giving all of your time is seen as a lack of commitment. If this is the case, then you may have to surrender some of your time, like it or not; but do your best to trim the required time to the bare minimum.

🕐 Stop being so generous with your time, and relearn the value of saying no when doing so is appropriate.

More Tips for Saying No

One key to saying no effectively is to develop what my colleague and fellow NSA board member Brian Tracy calls "Won't Power"—the power to declare and stick to all the things you *won't* do (I'm harking back to the *Not*-To-Do list I discussed in Chapter 1). It's a lot easier to say no and make it stick if you keep your own needs firmly in mind. Those *have* to come first! Remember this key aspect of the PWF process: reduce, reduce, reduce. If you don't put yourself at the head of your own line and block all comers, someone else will definitely cut ahead of you. To use another metaphor, this is *your* hill, and you have to remain king or queen of it.

You have the right to say no to any request you can't afford. Stand firm without being guilted into saying yes. Maybe you're the type of person who tries to do your best for everyone. But how likely are you to produce at your peak on a task you didn't want to take on in the first place? What if you've exceeded your physical or mental limits?

Your feelings matter. If you want to say no, there's a reason behind it. Sometimes, you simply have to listen to your own gut. With that in mind, here are some additional tips for saying no.

All you need is love. Do your best to say no in an upbeat way. I know this sounds like a contradiction in terms, but there's a big difference between saying "Not just no, but hell no," and "I'd love to but just can't take that on right now!" A positive rejection can ensure no one gets hurt feelings, especially if you follow up with, "But please keep me in mind for any further projects!" You're not making any promises, but you're keeping the lines of communication open. And thank the person for considering you in the first place, since you might need their help someday.

Don't make empty promises. If you can't do something (or just don't want to), come right out and say it. Don't make an empty promise and then let it come crashing down around you, leaving your requester in the lurch. If you turn them down flat, they have the opportunity to find someone else. If you find it uncomfortable to say no immediately, ask for a little time to think it over. This will put the person on notice you might very well refuse them. Then return with your answer promptly and politely.

Don't apologize for or explain yourself. If you can't take on a new task, decline without making an issue out of it and offering a ton of explanations. A simple, "Sorry—I'd love to help out, but I don't have the bandwidth right now," is sufficient. They don't need to know more; in any case, you're not obliged to justify yourself, no matter how much you might disappoint the other party. If someone insists on knowing why you needed to say no, diplomatically give them a brief truth, whatever the case may be: It's not in your skill set; you don't feel you can do the project justice; you don't have the time in your schedule; or you're saving the time for your family or something important to you. If someone really insists, firmly reiterate you can't do it. Be polite but assertive. This, of course, applies to fellow coworkers. For the boss, you'll need to try negotiation.

Negotiate. If your boss presents you with a task you can't outright refuse, but your plate is undeniably full, don't hesitate to point this out. Don't beat around the bush. Openly discuss your current deadlines and workload, and communicate both honestly and clearly. For example, you might say, "I'm currently working on X, Y, and Z projects. As things stand, I believe this additional project is beyond my capacity at the moment, and I want to return quality work in a timely way. Would you like me to hand it off to someone else, hire a contractor, or would you prefer to reprioritize my existing project load for me?" How you approach this, of course, depends on your circumstances, but it does put the ball back into your manager's court.

Meet someone halfway. Sometimes it's hard to say no to a request, especially when it's clear someone thinks enough of you to try to tap your expertise. While I feel it's critical for you to develop the capacity to refuse, you can arrange to meet people halfway and offer alternatives to immediately adding something to your HIT list. For example, you might admit you're already booked up, but make it clear you'll do all you can to help. Or, rather than being a committee member, you'll act in an advisory capacity. Perhaps you can't drop what you're juggling right now, but there's an open spot somewhere ahead in your schedule in a few weeks. Inform the requester you can do the task then, and not now. This solution may satisfy you both if the task isn't time-critical. If you really want to help with a new task, but you genuinely don't have the time, be honest and ask if there's some way you can contribute without going all-in.

Be persistent and consistent. Some people just won't take no for an answer and will keep bugging you to take on a task, no matter how many times you refuse them. In a case like this one, you'll have to respond to their persistence with persistence of your own. Now, I'm not talking about someone who responds to your rejection with a standard statement like, "Aw, are you sure? Well, if you change your mind . . ." Some people will feel obliged to ask a second time later on; again, this is no big deal if you just say no again. Use this technique with the dysfunctional ones who demand to know why not (see the first tip) or ask over and over, as if they can't believe you refused them. Don't let them wear you down.

Be crystal clear. Be straightforward when turning someone down; say no when you mean no. Don't couch your rejection in obscure terms or beat around the bush; just say no in a direct way, so you don't have to repeat yourself because you confused someone. Your answer should be clear to any reasonable person, and you don't need to argue.

Don't worry too much about their feelings. Some people take a turndown as a blow to their self-esteem. This is not your problem. Your goal is to reduce your commitment level, not to help others reduce theirs—and that's exactly what they're attempting when they ask you to take on their tasks. Don't let pity overwhelm your common sense; unless something awful and unfair has happened, you can't afford to feel sorry for everyone and everything. Just because they've let something blow up into a crisis doesn't mean it's your crisis—unless you take it on.

You Want a Piece of Me?

Everyone wants to be the nice person in the office . . . well, maybe not the curmudgeon over there in the corner. But you can take a cue from him, because he's not afraid to say no. You can't be afraid either, or others won't hesitate to lay claim to whatever pieces of your time they can grab. I assure you, once you become known as an "easy mark," people will tap you for help more and more often, until you're completely snowed under. That doesn't make you valuable—it makes you a sucker. So in the long run, it's a better idea to stick to your guns and learn to say no clearly, so you can maintain your workload (not to mention your sanity) at a viable level. Then you won't *become* the curmudgeon in the corner.

RESCUING YOUR TIME FROM MEETINGS

An important part of working in the professional world is collaboration and teamwork. Meetings, appointments, and conference calls are essential in making this happen. Unfortunately, meetings are among the worst time-stealers in corporate America. It seems that the more "important" (or higher-level) a person is within an organization's hierarchy, the more time is spent in meetings.

Unfortunately, many meetings really don't do much, other than use up valuable time. Exceptions exist, and some leaders run them well—but most do not. You'd have a hard time eliminating meetings entirely, since they're a staple in the corporate culture. However, if you're going to perform at your productive best, you definitely have to apply the "less is more" concept to meetings.

Less Time in Conference Rooms

You need to find a way to spend *more* time working and less time in meetings. You can accomplish just about everything done in a meeting more efficiently in another format. For example, you might use e-mail for status updates and report distribution. In fact, a well-crafted e-mail is often as effective as a sit-down meeting. So why do we waste our time with face time?

I do think in-person meetings have some valid uses. Work is done and decisions are made in meetings. They're helpful when introducing new people working together at the beginning of a project. Meetings are also valuable for hashing problems out, brainstorming, and making joint decisions—the only reason you may need to meet for more than a few minutes.

Otherwise, I'm about 90 percent convinced that the biggest reason people call meetings is so the meeting holder can feel important. I'm also about 90 percent convinced the biggest reason people attend those meetings is so *they* can feel important. After all, if you're invited to the meeting, you're important. Right?

As in so many other workplace situations, the simple word "no" truly comes in handy here. Let's try it out in a meeting invitation scenario:

> Bob: "Joe, I need you to come to the meeting on inter-departmental cooperation."
>
> Your answer: "Why?"
>
> Bob: "We need someone to represent your department's point of view."

Here it is, the perfect opportunity! Tell the meeting holder, "Thanks for asking me, but no. My schedule is already full. Can you e-mail me a synopsis afterward?"

Granted, this probably isn't going to work with your boss, but it probably *will* work in most other cases. Base your decisions on whether or not the meeting will help accomplish your goals. If it doesn't, why should you go?

The meetings you do attend should be results-oriented and limited in frequency. They must also stick to the stated agenda without going off on tangents. Before you step inside, decide how much time you can invest in the meeting, and make it clear to the other participants at the beginning. If the meeting runs over schedule, you're justified in leaving. At each meeting, strive to arrange for e-mail or telephone follow-up, rather than scheduling yet another meeting to report on your progress.

🕐 Rather than waste time on meetings, distribute necessary information via e-mail, phone calls, and other media.

Reducing Meeting Mania

Do you find it's nearly impossible to get five or more attendees together at the same time? When key players are overbooked, it can take hours just to schedule a single meeting. Here are three questions you should ask yourself before calling a meeting and inviting a bunch of people:

1. *Do we really need all these people?* Make sure you aren't inviting anyone who doesn't need to have a seat at the table. Not only does it make scheduling more difficult, but you'll either (a) waste others' time or (b) bend over backwards to accommodate someone who isn't going to show up anyway. Don't worry about hurting someone's feelings; they'll be thrilled to not have to attend.

2. *Can we keep people in the loop without inviting them to every meeting?* Some meetings are full of wallflowers who need to know what's going on but don't necessarily need to contribute. Publishing meeting minutes or distributing essential information electronically can save time and shorten the attendee list. Also, find out if some departments are sending multiple representatives. By choosing a single person from each department, you can make sure everyone is represented without having everyone in the room. Need some more incentive to drop people from the attendee list? Take the approximate hourly salary of each attendee and calculate the cost of the meeting. The meeting may cost thousands of dollars!

3. *Do we need to meet at all?* This is a question you should ask about every meeting, not just the hard-to-schedule ones. Any meeting that doesn't have a clear objective—or better yet, a formal agenda—should be on the chopping block.

Be selective about time-hungry commitments like meetings, so you can free up time for other priorities. Remember, our goal for this workflow process is to achieve more while doing less. This requires an active commitment to reducing the amount you do each day. Paring down your time spent in meetings will leave you with more time to tackle your HIT list—what really matters in the long run. The quicker you can attack your HIT list, the quicker you can call it a day and enjoy all the other things life has to offer.

IN THE DECISION COMES THE DILEMMA

When you're attempting to gain control of your time usage, it's often the little moments that count. Specifically, one moment: the second you think to yourself, "Okay . . . what should I do next?" In that space of time, you choose to be productive . . . or not.

We face many such moments in the course of each day. If someone cuts you off in traffic, you choose—in a split second—whether to flip him off or to apply the brake. If your partner is in a foul mood and says something snippy to you, you'll take a second to inhale and decide in that moment to decide whether to escalate the conversation or say something soothing. It doesn't matter whether you're angry or not; in fact, you probably still are. But you're going to make a purposeful choice about what to do next.

The same is true in time management. Think about the everyday decisions you make in a split second—decisions that would seem inconsequential if you thought about them at all, but that might lead you toward or away from using your time wisely. For example, do you:

- Open a word processor and write an impactful article for a blog, organization newsletter, or client . . . OR open Outlook and spend time messing around with your e-mail?
- Dive into that spreadsheet and do difficult brain work . . . OR pick up the phone and call a friend?
- Rehearse for an important presentation next week . . . OR research airfare options for your next vacation?

It's astonishingly easy to choose the unproductive option, simply because we're human. It's tempting to take a mental vacation and do a fun task, instead of the difficult one requiring brainpower and focus. However, the results are vastly different. On the one hand is a day filled with activity; on the other, a day filled with accomplishment. Remember, they're not necessarily synonymous.

Making the correct choice "in the moment" requires a three-step process:

1. *Clarity.* You have to know, in advance, what your priorities are for the day. Without a complete list of choices, you won't have an accurate answer to the question "what's next?" If you don't have a HIT list, any choice will get you "there," but "there" may actually be *nowhere.* If you already have a plan, you can execute toward it much more efficiently.

2. *Discernment.* Assuming you know your priorities, judgment is the next step. At the exact moment you choose which fork in the road to take, evaluate which alternative will result in a better outcome (P1–P4). Checkmarks on a list aren't equal; they have weight. If you could see results, one checkmark might look like a faint pencil mark, and another a broad stroke with a marker.

3. *Discipline.* Once you make a choice between alternatives, self-control determines the outcome. Do you actually follow through on your good decisions? If you told yourself, "I should work on my strategic plan," what would you do next: open the document, or open Facebook?

🕒 Before you take a break between tasks, consider how long that choice may take you away from your work—and how it will affect your momentum.

This three-step process can make the difference between a productive outcome, with results you're proud of, and an unproductive one, where you feel like banging your head against the wall for yet another wasted day. These decision dilemmas happen to us hundreds of times a day. Choose wisely!

SUMMARY: PWF STEP 2 CHECKUP

Once you've identified the critical few tasks you should focus on, you'll need to find the time to do them. This process requires careful scheduling, whereby you assign appropriate time slots and durations for each appointment and task. In addition, you must make decisions quickly, learn to say no to unwelcome work, and control your meetings.

Time management isn't really time management, but self-management—your willingness to stop misusing time in ways that limit your productivity. In pursuit of this effort, establish routines to help you keep moving forward, and set realistic deadlines to decide when and how to accomplish each task.

Once you've established a deadline for a particular task, calculate how much time you must work on the task each day. Then fit the time into your schedule according to the task's priority, using the triage system from Chapter 1. Emergencies and other crises aside, tasks generally fall into three scheduling categories:

- "Have-to" items required by your job
- Routine daily tasks
- Items from your HIT list

Further reduce your commitments in any way possible: by asking yourself and others, "How long will this take?" for each task; by applying the "availability caching" concept; and by turning down any work that you don't want or can't handle. Many of us have trouble turning people down, but you should learn to do so effectively, so people won't take advantage of you. Follow these guidelines:

- Say no in an upbeat, positive way.
- Don't make empty promises.
- Don't apologize or explain yourself.
- Negotiate as necessary.
- Meet the other person halfway.
- Be persistent and consistent.
- Be crystal clear.
- Don't worry about someone's feelings over your own needs.

Last, many meetings are unnecessary, so find ways to trim as many as you can out of your schedule, and let people know you're willing to do so. Finally, exercise clarity, discernment, and vision to make the correct choices "in the moment," so you don't waste valuable time by allowing yourself to be derailed between tasks.

3

Focus Your Attention

Once you've determined what to do and have scheduled time to complete it, you must concentrate on its completion. The most effective time management system in the world won't do a thing to improve your productivity if you don't focus on the critical tasks at hand. For many of us, the problem isn't a lack of willpower—it's having the restraint to refuse distractions.

More than ever, we modern workers are bedeviled by interruptions that pull us away, willingly or otherwise, from the key activities of our jobs. If it's not our noisy office-mates, it's the siren song of the Internet or an over-fascination with e-mail.

You must learn to concentrate on the truly important tasks. Wield your focus like a blade, stripping away anything that might keep you from getting your work done on time and under budget. This is where the rubber hits the road. You actually have to see each task through to completion, as hard as it may be.

In this chapter, I'll discuss the modern curse of workplace distractions, both external and internal, and show you how to face down and deal with these dangerous focus-stealers.

DRIVEN TO DISTRACTION

Distraction is an enemy to getting things done. When it finds its way into your life, a simple task can take hours, or can be lost in a sea of other tasks. Your distractions aren't necessarily bad things, but even good tasks done at the wrong time can keep you from your priorities and fill your schedule quickly.

Interruptions abound. A coworker drops by to chat, the phone rings, and your boss sends you an e-mail to handle something, pronto—all at the same time. With a flurry of activity, you respond to these various demands. All prove to be low priority, and an hour later, you return to your initial task, your energy waning. You decide you'll work on the project in the afternoon, when your energy picks up again. Of course, after lunch, there's some new crisis—and after fielding a volley of phone calls and unscheduled visits from coworkers, the day ends, and the project remains, yet again, unfinished.

When you lose your momentum, your brain has to work harder to get back up to speed, just like a car forced to come to a full stop. Although interruptions are a normal (and sometimes desirable) part of our work experience, there are times when it's helpful to defend against them.

You have to put on the blinders and shut out distractions of all kinds when you need to concentrate on a difficult task. This won't be easy, as distractions are constantly lurking, waiting to sneak into your life. To shut them out, focus your attention tightly on a specific task, one thing at a time, getting rid of all the distractions you can. You may require some new habits and possibly a change in your work environment.

Ultimately, the problem here is twofold: external and internal. Let's take a look at both kinds of distractions and how to handle them, starting with the external type.

HANDLING EXTERNAL DISTRACTIONS

It's hard to accomplish much when someone's bugging you. According to a recent study, an amazing 28 percent of the average worker's day is spent dealing with interruptions caused by others and then trying to recapture lost focus.[11] However, other people aren't necessarily aware of your need for quiet, uninterrupted workflow—and many just don't care. They get caught up in their own concerns and forget to be considerate, thus damaging your productivity in the process.

Stop people from deliberately taking up your time when you need to get work done. Shut out their incidental noise and movements as well. To do this, cut yourself off from the rest of the world as much as possible.

Granted, it's easy to insulate yourself if you're in upper management and have an office with a door and a staff to filter out the inconsequential. But even if you don't, you can arrange your workspace so you're not constantly derailed by interruptions and distractions. At the very least, if you have a door, get up and close it; lock it if necessary. This will not only soundproof things a bit, it'll keep many people from actively bothering you. For the clueless, hang up a "Do Not Disturb" sign.

The above assumes you have a door; these days, many of us don't. If you've ever worked in an open-plan office, you know cubicles provide plenty of distraction. Listening in on the conversation in the next cubicle, watching people walk by, and hearing the clicking fingernails of the gal typing across the way are common cubicle distractions.

In such a circumstance, isolating yourself may mean finding an out-of-the-way office, moving temporarily into an empty conference room, taking your laptop to the break room, or plopping down on a bench outdoors where you can work for a while in peace.

If you want or need to stay in your office, try these options:

- Turn your workspace away from active areas like busy hallways.

🕐 Don't allow people to hold conversations outside your cubicle or office door. Politely but firmly shoo them away so you can get your work done, and don't worry about what they think.

- Listen to soothing music or ambient noise to drown out incidental sounds.
- Wear noise-canceling or noise-attenuating earphones while you do the above. People might think you're listening to something and might be less likely to interrupt you.
- Set up a signal to let people know you need to work uninterrupted. For example, you might wear a red cap when you're deep into something and need to concentrate.
- Set a symbolic barrier across your doorway, such as police tape or a cube door.[12]
- Hold off on responding to e-mails; close your e-mail program to give yourself some time to focus.
- Send your calls directly to voicemail, so the ringing doesn't distract you.
- Turn off your cell phone (don't just set it to vibrate).

Finally, if your office uses shared scheduling software like Microsoft Outlook, you can also create a virtual "blackout" period by scheduling an appointment on your calendar. Anyone checking your schedule will see you're busy, and they're less likely to schedule a conflicting meeting time.

The Bottom Line

I don't care if you have to hide out, put earplugs in your ears and blinders on your glasses, or hang a "Go Away" sign on the door—get rid of those external distractions! What if your co-worker thinks you're ignoring him to get your work done? So what! You're the one who's being productive. When the boss is passing out raises and promotions, your productivity will make a difference.

⏱ If you can't escape the distractions in your office, explore the possibility of telecommuting a day or two from home each week.

HEADING OFF INTERNAL DISTRACTIONS

Once you've dealt with the external distractions, work on weeding out the internal ones—the ones your own mind creates. They're much more insidious than their external kindred. While you can usually isolate yourself from other distractions, you can't get away from YOU. As the saying goes, no matter where you go, there you are.

If you ever expect to escape the distraction cycle, exercise your self-discipline first, last, and always. Put your shoulder to the wheel, and make the conscious decision to work hard even when there are distractions galore—especially when you don't feel like it. You'll be amazed at how much you can get done if you just push through the malaise and desire to be distracted; after a while, you'll probably get into the groove and forget you were tempted in the first place.

Take a good look at your workday, and make a conscious effort to eliminate the activities and behaviors sucking your day away. Remember: reduce, reduce, reduce! You won't even miss many of these time-wasters once they're gone.

Now, saying all this is easy enough; but how do you do it? Start by learning your own weaknesses and make rules to control them. Be aggressive about it! Ask yourself: What must I *stop* doing in order to become more productive? Here are a number of suggestions (you can add some of these to your *Not-To-Do* list):

- Stop negative self-talk.
- Limit workplace socializing.
- Refuse to participate in office politics if at all possible.
- Don't waste work time updating your résumé or job hunting.
- Quit arriving late and leaving early.
- Avoid excessively long lunches (unless they're work-related).
- Limit your use of social media, even for business purposes.
- Quit taking so many smoke breaks.

• Don't take too many brief breaks in general, because they derail your train of thought.

We often shoot ourselves in the foot in terms of productivity; the points listed above provide only a general outline of what not to do. Now, let's talk a closer look at some additional points I consider the most problematic for concentration.

Multitasking

Everybody's trying to do more in less time these days. We've become a world of multitasking mavens, checking e-mail on one computer screen while video-conferencing on a second, and scrambling to finish an important report on the third. We can take calls, answer e-mails, and check information with the click of a button. Smartphones and other electronic devices allow us to bring our work lives with us everywhere we go.

Ask yourself, "Has multitasking turned me into the human equivalent of a hamster running on an exercise wheel?" If so, you know how it feels: You're zipping along but not really getting anywhere.

Is multitasking *really* productive? As it turns out, there's no simple yes-or-no answer to this question. Overall, the outlook for multitasking doesn't seem especially positive, although it does have its good points. According to a 2006 study by Cornell University psychologist Morten Christiansen and National Institutes of Health research fellow Christopher Conway, most people can multitask just fine as long as they devote different senses to different tasks.[13] In other words, most of us have no problem listening to the radio while driving, or talking on the phone while taking a walk or chopping veggies. Sounds like a win for multitasking, right?

But similar stimuli tend to jam up our frequencies, because they compete for the same senses at the same time. Think about how you react when two people try to talk to you at once; you can't really understand either, can you? When you try, your brain bogs down and you have to expend a tremen-

🕐 Stop multitasking. It just dilutes your attention and fools you into thinking you're productive, when you're really just busy.

dous amount of energy just to concentrate. The same thing can happen when you try to focus on two or more technologies at once, especially if they're too similar: for example, voicemail and e-mail.

Furthermore, a study by researchers Joshua Rubinstein, David Meyer, and Jeffrey Evans, reported in the *Journal of Experimental Psychology: Human Perception and Performance* back in 2001, showed that switching between complex tasks actually causes us to lose several seconds of time for each switch.[14] Think about it. How many times do you change tasks in a day? Several hundred? If you're really trying to multitask, it may be several *thousand* times a day. A few seconds several thousand times a day adds up to some significant time. Let's say you end up shifting focus two thousand times a day for just two seconds per shift. That totals to four thousand seconds, which is over one hour you could be spending on other things!

Rubenstein et al. have proposed a new model to explain this mental shifting process. The first step is "goal shifting," where you make a conscious decision to change from working on one task to the other. The second step is "rule activation," where you wipe your short-term memory of the data and procedures for the first task and replace it with the data and procedures for the new task. The more complex or unfamiliar the task, the more time you need to accomplish the rule activation.

For biological reasons, most of us can absorb and integrate only so much input at once, complicating the rule activation aspect of paying attention. We literally have a limited amount of attention we can dole out. You can't develop a productive focus when you're trying to do more than one important thing at once. If you try to handle the classic multitasking job of walking and chewing gum at the same time, you may not have much trouble with reprogramming your rule activation on the fly. Both of the above are simple tasks you're accustomed to doing, and because those tasks are simple, they tend to fade into the background. But that isn't the case for high-level tasks requiring constant processing of new information.

Consider cell phones and cars. Although most of us do it, we know it's foolish to talk on the phone and drive at the same time. Because both tasks require such a high investment of cognitive resources and constant, overlapping rule activation, they detract from each other. As a result, we do one or the other poorly—or more likely, both. The high number of phone-related car accidents is proof enough of this. The National Safety Council estimates that cell phones caused 1.3 *million* car crashes in 2011 alone (that's down from 1.6 million in 2010).[15] So imagine how ineffective it is to simultaneously try to work on a report, chat online, sing along with Carrie Underwood, check your favorite news website, and respond to e-mail. There's never an opportunity to drop into the kind of productive focus that gets the job done efficiently.

All the things we're trying to multitask on have another name: interruptions. Whether those interruptions come from others or we create them in our own minds, they're still interruptions. We have to stop what we're doing in order to do something else. You can't work effectively with stop-and-go thought processes, any more than you can get anywhere swiftly in stop-and-go traffic. No matter how smart you are, trying to do more than a few things at once will just destroy your ability to focus effectively.

While multitasking may be in vogue these days, it simply isn't as productive as forcing yourself to pay attention to one thing at a time to the exclusion of everything else. You'll get more done by applying a laser focus to one task, completing it, and then moving on to the next task. Trying to tackle too much at once just leads to a greater potential for distraction and a longer time to task completion.

So concentrate on one thing at a time, because attention

is meant to be undivided. You can't afford to distract yourself with multitasking, especially when you already have to deal with distractions from others.

Procrastination

We've all let things slide when we shouldn't have. It's not always about forgetfulness, or overwork, or even laziness. In fact, some of the worst procrastinators are busy professionals who are otherwise successful in the workplace. But procrastination generates anxiety and negativity, so why do we hobble ourselves this way? The reasons are rarely clear-cut, but often they consist of some mix of the following:

- Lack of self-confidence
- Uncertainty about who can help
- Perfectionism
- Distractions
- Fear of failure
- Time pressure
- Anger or hostility toward the task
- Low frustration tolerance
- Indecision on what to do next

We tend to put off the unpleasant (or potentially unpleasant) tasks, no matter how high their value. What can you do to stop procrastination in its tracks? Try these options.

Visualize. There are two basic kinds of motivation, and you can use both in your visualization scheme. First of all, consider the positive: Visualize having a lingering task completed and out the door. What kinds of wonderful things will result? Second, negative visualization can work, too. From personal experience, you *know* unpleasant things rarely go away if you ignore them. They just get worse. If you let an unfinished task fester on your HIT list, it gobbles up your mental resources, to your detriment.

🕐 If you break down a large task into subtasks
in order to overcome procrastination, make sure
you set deadlines and internal milestones for each
of the subtasks, and track them carefully.

Strategize. If you have trouble getting started with a big task, try breaking the task into smaller chunks. For example, a twenty-hour project might break down into ten two-hour subtasks. Forget waiting for a "block of time." Such a thing no longer exists. The key is to *do something* to move toward completion. So ask yourself, "What is the single next action step I'd need to take to see forward progress on this project?" Get to work, and plan how you're going to tackle each individual subtask; if it helps, sketch it out on paper. Put those subtasks on your HIT lists; if someone doesn't do it for you, set deadlines for each, along with an overall timeline for when you have to have the whole task completed.

Eliminate distractions. How can you get anything done if you're always checking your e-mail, answering your cell phone, or surfing the Internet? If you're easily distracted, get rid of the distractions until you make some headway on the task. Unplug the landline, turn off your cell phone, disable the Internet, and forget you even have e-mail!

Get busy. Assuming you have all the information and resources required to move forward, action always beats meditation. Once you've given the task enough thought, leap into action. Focus like a laser on your task. If you have to, grit your teeth and tell yourself, "I'm going to do this, like it or not!"

With some tasks, you simply have to put your head down and bull on through. No, it's probably not fun; but then again, we wouldn't call it work if it was fun. Onerous tasks need your attention at least as much as the fun stuff. Even if you do it a little at a time, eventually you'll get the monster task off your plate, so your boss will stop growling about it, and you can stop stewing about it.

Perfectionism

While a desire for perfection is admirable, it becomes increasingly difficult the closer you get to the goal. At some point, you have to decide you've done what you can and it's good enough. No, I'm not advocating laziness or sloppiness. I'm the first to admit that perfectionism indicates a desire for excellence, sets a high standard for achievement, and encourages us to do our best in all things.

However, true perfection is in the realm of the divine; it's just not going to happen very often here on Earth. If you expect perfection in everything, you'll never be happy—or as productive—because you're hung up on getting it right instead of getting it *done*. A quest for perfection can paralyze you; even if it doesn't, there's absolutely no way you can stay properly focused on the few important things if you're agonizing over little details.

Let's see if you're letting your inner perfectionist take over. Do you:

- Always run at 110 percent capacity?
- Leave no room for error?
- Criticize yourself constantly?
- Expect too much from others?
- Get depressed if goals go unmet?
- Feel a constant fear of failure?

🕐 Rather than let perfectionism paralyze you, get to work and figure out the details as you go along.

- Get defensive when criticized, even constructively?
- Have low self-esteem?
- Wait until everything's perfect before starting a task?

If most of these points describe you, then, to paraphrase comic Jeff Foxworthy, you might be a perfectionist.

Too much perfectionism can be detrimental to your productivity. Good enough usually *is* good enough, especially on the first pass. Here are some tips for taming the beast of perfectionism:

- Step back and take a look at the bigger picture.
- Set realistic expectations.
- Establish deadlines for yourself.
- Give yourself permission to be imperfect.
- Stop comparing yourself to others.
- Give yourself credit for what you do right.
- Accept criticism as intended.
- Focus on what you're doing now, not on past mistakes or future worries.
- Learn to relax.
- Quit waiting for the perfect conditions and get started.
- Ask for help when you need it.

Yes, you should try to be the best you can be. In fact, you can harness your perfectionist tendencies as a motivational tool—without taking them so far they start causing problems. Do your best within your time constraints; then, if you have extra time to work on something, go back and kick it up a notch. If not, stop worrying. Just keep reminding yourself: Productivity is more important than perfection any day.

Negative Self-Talk

Each of us goes through life constantly thinking about and internally commenting on the situations we encounter. This self-talk helps us manage our reactions and decide what to do next. Unfortunately, self-talk can be self-defeating. If you convince yourself something's too difficult or there's no point in trying, you throw roadblocks in the path of productivity. Negative self-talk is a prime component of procrastination, and it can also contribute to perfectionism—for example, if you keep telling yourself you've got to do something just right or else—you'll become paralyzed as a result.

You've got to get a handle on negative self-talk before it leads you into the Slough of Despond and ruins your productivity. The best thing to do is to dispute it all the way down the line. Give yourself a reality check: Are your facts straight? What evidence do you have for your negativity? Are you jumping to conclusions? Next, put it all in perspective by challenging your self-talk:

- Is the situation really as bad as it seems?
- If so, what's the worst that could happen?
- How about the best thing?
- What's most likely to occur?
- How would I perceive this situation if I were in a positive mood?

It's difficult to eliminate self-sabotage in all of its forms, since many of us tend to be our own worst critics. But in order to be productive, you have to be realistic and ruthless about facing down your subconscious.

☺ If you ever find yourself thinking you can't possibly accomplish a task, challenge that negative self-talk instantly, put your head down, and forge ahead.

SLIPPING THE ELECTRONIC LEASH

The distractions associated with electronic technology can be either internal or external—and on most days, they're both. Either way, they can cause shocking damage to your productivity level.

Electronic technology *can* be a boon to productivity; it does make life easier in some ways. Nowadays, it's easy to contact just about anyone at the touch of a button. You can accomplish tasks almost anywhere, during what would otherwise be unusable downtime. With access to the Internet, even doing research is a snap, whether you're sitting in a Starbucks or in your corner office.

E-mail, cell phones, handhelds, iPads, and the like are supposed to be tools to maximize your productivity; they shouldn't control your behavior. But somehow, many of us have gotten to the point where we're terrified to disconnect even for a moment, just in case we miss something. When the incoming message alert chimes, we drop what we're doing to check it, like Pavlov's dogs drooling when the bell rings. Worse, we're like dogs on leashes, pulled this way and that, whether we like it or not. We allow our technology—particularly our electronic devices—to dictate our actions, often to our detriment. We let them exhaust us, making us forgetful, distracted, and often rude.

Here's an extreme example. One of my clients, the vice president of a large telecommunications company, was visiting a client with one of his sales representatives. They were all sitting in the client's office having their business meeting when the salesman's BlackBerry went off. The salesman immediately pulled it out, tapped around, and started typing a response, not saying anything to the other two people. The VP quickly took over the conversation, and continued the client meeting without the rep's input. Eventually, the salesman finished typing, and he rejoined the meeting.

Afterward, the VP asked him, "Wow, is everything okay?"

The salesman replied, "What do you mean?"

"You interrupted a meeting and answered a message on your BlackBerry. Clearly, it must have been very important," the VP said.

"Oh, not really; it was a client wondering if I had time to see him in two weeks," the sales rep explained. "I've created an expectation of responsiveness with my clients."

The VP was dumbfounded! The sales rep was so addicted to his handheld he couldn't pay attention to the client sitting right in front of him. Talk about cutting off your nose to spite your face! The VP made a mandate that day that all handhelds had to be completely powered down whenever anyone entered a meeting with a client.

In order to avoid this self-inflicted ADHD and become truly productive, slip the electronic leash. In other words, harness your toys rather than letting them harness you: Internet, social media, handheld devices, e-mail, texting, and the like. These are tools, so treat them as such—not as demanding little bosses constantly crying out for your attention. Why should you let them dictate to you? Learn to use these tools for what they're intended, and exercise some thoughtfulness about when it's acceptable to use them . . . and when it isn't. Choose for yourself when it's time to check them.

The solution to electronic overwhelm is simple: When you're trying to concentrate, turn off and tune out. Deactivate all beeps, lights, flashes, noises, and notifications. Kill the incoming message alerts on your e-mail, chat clients, and social media. Let those phone calls roll over to voicemail. This is another case where, in the long run, less is more. Sure, most

---

⏱ Turn off your electronic devices before you attend client meetings. It's too easy to let electronics distract you during face time.

of us need to stay in touch in order to get our jobs done, but who says you have to answer every message as soon as it comes in? There's very little you have to attend to instantly, unless you're a trauma surgeon. Nothing enters your life in priority order anyway.

You have only so much energy, so you can't waste it on trivial things like answering messages the moment they appear. You need to concentrate on your important tasks, without letting distractions yank you away from what really matters. No matter how minor the interruption, it takes time to refocus and get back into the flow, so your productivity is undeniably affected.

A Dangerous Disease

Back in 2009, I introduced the concept of Obsessive-Compulsive Social Media Disorder (OCSMD). As the name suggests, OCSMD is associated primarily with compulsively checking Facebook and obsessively tweeting away on Twitter, but I think it's applicable for electronic media of any kind, including e-mail and texting. E-mail is especially bad, in my opinion. It's no longer an event, or out of the ordinary in any sense; now it's background noise. We respond instantly and no longer realize we do it; so it controls us, and we sit there waiting for the next message to come in.

Rather than allow yourself to get distracted—exactly what you're doing when you stay constantly connected—set aside blocks of time when you can receive and answer your messages all at once, whether via e-mail or telephone. You can do it a few times a day for thirty or sixty minutes at a time. That way, you can focus on getting your professional interactions taken care of all at once, without letting them defocus you throughout the day.

Short of completely eschewing this technology—no longer a reasonable option—you have to set real, solid strictures on its use. You're not a machine. You can't always be on, and you certainly shouldn't stay connected when you should be re-charging. Truly productive people realize the need to disconnect from the world occasionally, whether that means taking brief breaks, spending evenings enjoying life, or going on vacation. Given enough rest, completely disconnected from your electronics, you can accomplish more when you *are* connected. When you refuse to set boundaries to limit your use of electronic technology, you're setting yourself up to fail. You may still function, but you'll never achieve your full potential.

To recapture your productive techno-edge, start small. Disconnect for a half-hour a day first, and then stretch it to an hour. At lunchtime, step away from your desk, turn off your BlackBerry, and leave the building. Sit in the park. Go out to eat. Visit with a friend. Get to know a colleague better. In other words, do the directly social things humans have done for 99.9 percent of our history.

Your electronic tools are intended to help you boost your production. That's it. Ultimately, they work for you. So to maintain your productive edge—and your sanity—never let yourself work for them.

FOCUS AIDS

Superior focus requires the ability to determine what matters and the determination to stick with it until you're done. Fortunately, aside from rooting out time-wasters and turning your back on distractions, there are other tools you can apply to maximize your focus. Let's take a look at a few.

If You Think It, Ink It!

The first time I heard my father utter what I came to think of as his signature phrase, I was standing ankle-deep in the Gulf of Mexico, catching baby jellyfish.

Catching jellyfish is very serious business when you're six years old. We were vacationing at Corpus Christi, Texas, after visiting family in nearby San Antonio, and this was my way of communing with the sea and, more important, Keeping Busy. Plus, I had to show those jellyfish who was boss.

Daddykins (my pet name for my father) was standing in the surf with his pants rolled up, watching closely as I captured jellyfish in my little bucket and took them a dozen feet down the shoreline to start a new life. He was crouching close, pointing out a new victim, when he straightened and looked absentmindedly toward the horizon for a moment. Then he reached into his shirt pocket for a pen and the little notepad he called his "brain" (I didn't understand back then how you could keep your brain in your pocket). He scribbled with a pen for a minute, flipped the notebook closed, put both back in his pocket, and went back to helping me with my task.

I'd seen him do that before, so this time I asked him, "Daddykins, what did you do just now?"

He replied matter-of-factly, "If you think it, ink it!"

That was the first of hundreds of times I'd hear him say that phrase in my lifetime. It meant, every time you think of something, write it down. Daddykins called himself "The Absentminded Professor," and if he *didn't* write something down the minute he thought of it, he'd forget it. If we were out at a restaurant or visiting friends and an idea struck him, out would come the paper "brain" and a pen. Moments later, after some quick scribbling, he'd snap it shut and mumble to whoever was in earshot, "If you think it, ink it!"

I'd roll my eyes and quickly change the subject. At that young age, I had no idea the impact the phrase would have on me. Obviously, at some point my father's lesson sank in, and thank goodness it did. Capturing ideas like this is critical for the busy professional, because (a) it helps you save minutes later on, since you don't have to try to remember an idea you didn't write down; (b) you can use forced downtime (when you're in a line, a waiting room, or traveling) to brainstorm; and (c) it keeps you on task, so you don't interrupt yourself to follow the shiny object when you're supposed to be focused on something more significant.

I think the last reason is the most important of the three, and it's certainly the most germane to this discussion. Whenever you capture a thought, your brain thinks you *did* whatever it was you were thinking about. You no longer have to expend mental energy remembering it or worrying about forgetting it, so you can go back to the task at hand. When you write down the thoughts interrupting your work flow, you're essentially setting them aside until you have the time to focus on them.

So when you have a random thought that sounds good, capture it right away. You can use a little notebook like my father's shirt-pocket "brain," a Day-Timer like the one I designed,[16] a handheld device like a BlackBerry, a compact voice recorder, 3 × 5 index cards, Microsoft Outlook, an Internet-based HIT list, your iPad—whatever works for you (we'll talk through more organizing ideas in Chapter 4). Once you've recorded your idea, your brain will think you've done something about it and stop bugging you, so you can focus. Even if your idea is of the non-bugging kind, if you write it down, you've recorded it in black and white. By "inking" it, you've made it real.

By the time you review your notes, you may have forgotten the idea altogether, so what you find may pleasantly surprise you. And what do you end up with? A list of things to do at some point. The best of your ideas move on to your Master list. Then you prioritize them, and eventually they end up on your HIT list, so you can focus your attention on them properly. And if you come up with another brilliant idea while you're working on your new tasks, well . . . if you think it, ink it!

⊕ If you don't already have a voice recorder
app on your smartphone, get one, so you can
capture ideas as they occur to you.

Memory Lists

What if you think of something you don't necessarily need to "do" but just need to remember? Some information isn't necessarily actionable: it's based on recall. Memory lists are perfect for grouping "don't forget" items. For example, if your friend told you about a great restaurant she visited, would you be able to remember the name four months later, just when you and your spouse were deciding where to eat? If your mom rented a movie she highly recommends, will you be able to recall the name the next time you're selecting a flick? What if it's your friend's birthday, but you absolutely cannot remember the perfect gift you thought of two months ago? Reminders aren't necessarily things you need to track on your to-do list. In fact, you don't know when you'll do them since you're not sure when you'll need the information again—they are contextual.

Here are some examples of the Memory lists I currently track:

- Article ideas
- Blog topics
- Birthdays
- Books to read
- Bus stop info
- Errands
- Gift ideas
- Groceries
- Honey-do's
- Passwords
- Projects
- Restaurants to try
- Shopping list
- Speech ideas
- Teachers
- Vacation ideas

- Videos to rent
- Wines to try
- Wish list

Any list your brain can imagine, you can and should track! You can track this using the Notes function in Outlook (the digital equivalent of a sticky note); a blank piece of paper with the list name filed behind the appropriate A-Z tab in your planner; with an online program like Remember the Milk; or an iPhone app.[17]

Combating Sounds with Sounds . . . or Silence

We all know how difficult it is to concentrate when it's noisy. But that begs a question: What exactly qualifies as noise? After all, you may barely notice what might drive me to distraction. In any case, one's ability to tolerate noise can vary according to health or mood. It's a lot easier to ignore your cubicle mate's loud talking if you're feeling fine and things are looking rosy . . . but imagine how annoyed you'd be if your allergies were acting up or your computer just crashed.

We've all been there, and we all know distracting noises can affect our productivity. But you might be surprised, and possibly shocked, by how much this is true. According to sound expert Julian Treasure, most people are one-third as productive in a noisy room as in a quiet one.[18] Assuming he's correct, then if you normally earn the organization $1,000 a day in a loud workplace, you could do $3,000 worth of business if you worked in relative silence.

True silence is rare, of course, so the best defense against annoying noise is distance. In the modern office, you're unlikely to have the option; lacking volume controls for your coworkers (wouldn't that be great!), you have little choice but to try to mask distracting noise. As I noted earlier in this chapter, listening to music with a top-notch pair of noise-reduction earphones is an effective technique. Be careful about songs with lyrics, though, because half the time you end up singing along (not very productive, unless you're Miley Cyrus).

This is where so-called "ambient noise" comes into play. Strictly defined, ambient noise is just about anything you'd expect to hear in the background of life: dogs barking, cars passing, distant voices, the dishwasher, the whoosh of the air conditioner. Productivity experts, however, define ambient noise as soothing, quiet, often cyclic recordings that create a "sonic space" allowing the kind of purposeful focus that heightens productivity. Wind through trees, rainfall, the soft rush of waves on the seashore, even gentle music—all have been touted as productivity boosters. But do they actually work?

The jury's still out on that. Despite some wild claims, ambient noise probably won't boost your productivity much. Some researchers have documented productivity increases as high as 6.3 percent in workers exposed to ambient noise; others believe pure silence is better.[19] On the other hand, as I've already pointed out, pure silence isn't going to happen in the modern office space—so anything masking background noise can certainly distract you from the distractions, as it were.

Whether or not sound can spike creativity, some sounds are certainly calming. At about twelve cycles per minute, for example, the sound of the seashore comes pretty close to the breathing cycling of a sleeping human. Both tend to comfort us, and birdsong also tends to relax us.

What some people find soothing acoustically is as individual as one's taste in clothing or food. Sure, most of us do like quiet, rushing sounds like the beach or falling water . . . but

---

🕑 When working, listen only to music you're thoroughly familiar with. Otherwise, you'll focus too much on the music and not on your work.

where does this leave the many students who study quite happily and effectively while blasting rock 'n' roll on the stereo? That's the type of ambient sound that allows them to maximize their productive potential. Apparently, they're not really listening to the music—they're just drowning out the noises that bug them.

So "soothing" is in the ear of the beholder. Heaven help 'em, there are probably people who find the sounds of an open-plan office restful.

All that said, I do think ambient noise is worth trying, but you can't assume that what works for others will work for you. If classical music puts you to sleep (definitely a productivity downer), do a little experimenting and see what you come up with. You may even find the most productive ambient noises—to steal a classic song lyric from Simon and Garfunkel—are the sounds of silence.

In that vein, I have a little mind trick I use to combat distraction, courtesy of Maxwell Smart of *Get Smart* fame, and it's goofy enough to make me really visualize it: I go into my "Cone of Silence." I say to myself, "Okay, I'm in my Cone now." It's often better to manage yourself than to try to manage others, I've learned over time. Create a bubble of silence around yourself, with everything turned off, and noise-canceling headphones on. Now you can work, even on a plane.

The Metacognitive Edge

Metacognition, literally "thinking about thinking," is an excellent defense against distraction. How does it work? Simple enough: You use your knowledge about the way you think to shape your behavior. Basically, you keep your focus issues and your tendency toward distraction in mind, and apply everything you've learned in this chapter—and anything else you think may work—to head distractions off at the pass while fine-tuning your focus.

No one knows you as well as you do; if you'll just be honest about that knowledge and use it to your advantage, you can become more self-regulated and less distracted by the unimportant.

Learning to focus properly requires more self-reliance, and thus more metacognitive effort, than most workplace tasks; that's a given, so just accept it and move on. No matter how sloppy a thinker you believe you are, you can force yourself to focus—*if* you're willing to apply self-discipline. You have to be constantly on the ball, thinking about what it takes to narrow your focus to the few things that really count, and putting what you discover into play.

Yes, it's painful; and yes, it may be quite a while before you completely master your focus. But it's worth the effort when you can, at will, invoke what author Winifred Gallagher calls "the cobra feeling" in her book *Rapt: Attention and the Focused Life*: "An almost muscular, albeit mental, bearing-down on a subject or object, which you rise above, hood flaring to block distractions, and hold steady in your unblinking focus."

All it takes is a serious commitment to removing distractions and interruptions from your cognitive path. Easy to say, hard to do—but remarkably rewarding in the end.

A Few More Words About Socializing

Learning to achieve a state of extreme focus, and applying it diligently in the workplace, can be a tough row to hoe. It's challenging as you try to break habits, and you don't want to end up suffering socially and getting labeled as unfriendly or distant. Some social interaction is required to ensure the smooth functioning of any organization.

So don't just shut everyone out all the time; realize socializing has an appropriate time and place. If you have a P1 task on your plate, you have no time to socialize until it's complete. But there's lunchtime, breaks, and the "twilight time" before and after work to rub elbows and be friendly with your coworkers. You can get to know them better when you're involved in team-building exercises, or take the time to do so offline, away from work. You can still be nice and get more than your share of work done.

Even so, other people might not like your attitude, labeling you as cold, standoffish, or not a team player; but if you don't answer to them, then what they think shouldn't matter to you much. All that really matters is how productive you are during the time you're at work and that you get incredible results in the time you're there. This gets you recognition at work and out of the office on time to be with your loved ones. You can be buddies with your coworkers at lunch later in the week.

The workday is for working; the rest of your life is for socializing and taking care of yourself and your family. The more you keep your professional and social lives from bleeding over into each other, the easier it will be.

🕐 You needn't become a social pariah just because you'd rather work than socialize. Consider arranging lunch dates or social outings outside of work hours so you can stay in touch with your coworkers.

THE ZEN OF AVOIDING DISTRACTION

Your brain is an incredibly capable computer. But just like the computer sitting on your desk, it's plagued by the old problem of "garbage in, garbage out." As long as you let the garbage of distractions and interruptions interfere with your work, you'll contaminate your output with garbage as well, thereby damaging your productive potential. So do everything you can to filter the incoming garbage out.

In particular, fight your natural tendency toward involuntarily paying attention to things that pop up suddenly. Evolution made sure we respond this way, and for good reason. Your body is programmed to react to the snake hissing at your feet, the wolf rushing at you, the eagle swooping in front of you, or the bug on your arm. Is it any wonder you're distracted by an e-mail alert, a coworker talking loudly on a speakerphone, or someone walking by? Of course not! But keep working on suppressing your tendency toward focusing on those things, in favor of a voluntary focus on what matters.

While distractions are inevitable, there *are* ways to reduce them. I've spent most of this chapter outlining strategies for doing so. Whatever you choose to implement, never lose sight of this crucial fact: Your boss or client is paying you for the very best you can give them. Don't cheat them, and don't cheat yourself.

All in all, push everything aside you possibly can, concentrate, and remain undeterred in your work. This lets you think more clearly, and fall into a "productive trance," allowing you to chew up tasks and spit out finished work at a surprising rate.

There's a time for work and a time for fun, and you can't do both effectively at the same time—not and accomplish anything worthwhile. So when you're at work, focus, focus, focus on what matters. Proper focus, like any other skill, requires discipline and mastery to achieve; so learn what distracts you, and then ruthlessly find ways to lessen or eliminate those distractions. Then act like a postage stamp and stick to one thing until you reach your destination. You'll be amazed at how much you can get done when you actually see a task through to completion—and how good you'll feel.

SUMMARY: PWF STEP 3 CHECKUP

You can achieve true productivity only when you hone your ability to focus to razor sharpness.

For most of us, distractions represent our biggest productivity hurdles. External distractions are bad enough, but at least you can escape from most of those: for example, by closeting yourself away from others, by establishing signals letting people know when they shouldn't disturb you, and by ignoring e-mail and phone calls until you have time to deal with them.

Internal distractions are much more insidious, since your own mind creates them—and you can't easily escape yourself. Self-discipline is your watchword here. Look closely at your workday, determine which activities waste your time, and make rules to control them. Enforce those rules aggressively, especially guarding against the following activities:

- Multitasking
- Procrastinating
- Perfectionism
- Negative self-talk
- Socializing

Taken together, these things can steal hours from your workday. The worst culprit may be multitasking, because it fools you into thinking you've accomplished a lot, when you've really just kept yourself busy. Instead of haphazardly trying to do ten things at once, focus on one activity until you've completed it, and then move on to the next one.

Too many of us jump whenever our smartphones, handhelds, e-mail, and other techno-tools tell us to, and we pay for it with lapses in productivity. If you've fallen prey to this habit, slip the electronic leash. Constant connection to the info-world can damage your productivity.

Enlist focus aids to help you maintain the thread of your daily productivity. Write down or otherwise record ideas as they occur to you, so you don't interrupt yourself to pursue a shiny new thought when you should be doing something else. Harness metacognition to help you understand how you think, so you can better head off distractions while fine-tuning your focus; and if you think it may help, try ambient sound to insulate you from external distraction.

4

Process New Information

When you're focused on completing a critical task within a specific amount of time, you want to access exactly what you need to support your work, exactly when you want it. You especially need to be able to retrieve all the information you require. But with multiple pieces of important data spread across twenty different documents and platforms covering the same general topic, how do you stay organized?

In this chapter, I'll show you. I'll begin by providing guidelines for reducing information, researching effectively, and reading efficiently. Then we'll discuss setting up a basic filing schema. I'll then explain how to refine your personal time management system for maximal efficiency. Once we cover the systems for organizing incoming information, I'll show you how to process each piece as it arrives with my original 6-D System for processing workflow inputs, whether by e-mail, paper, or voicemail. This methodology will help you make quick decisions and get information into the right place, so you can access it immediately.

TAMING THE INFORMATION GLUT

Each day, you have to sift through a ton of available information to find the few things you really need. It's far too easy to overdose—when you take in so much information, you don't have time to process it all. Unprocessed information doesn't accomplish anything, since any new information has to mesh with your understanding and methodology before it's applicable. Therefore, to make the best use of the information available, be selective about what you accept. Let's consider some ways you can do that.

Reduce the Inflow

First of all, do everything in your power to reduce the amount of information crossing your desk in the first place. In the modern office, receiving too much e-mail is a particular problem, and processing your inbox can be a nerve-racking experience. If you're fortunate enough to have an assistant, put that person in charge of screening your e-mail. An assistant's biggest responsibility is to save you time, and this is one of the best ways to do it.

If an assistant isn't in the picture, establish e-mail filters or rules to limit the amount of e-mail you receive. First, install a spam-blocker so you don't have to deal with unwanted commercial e-mail (or diligently train the one your company has installed for you). Look at each message you receive and weigh it for its value. Does e-mail from a particular source really help you get your job done? If the source sometimes sends you useful e-mails but sometimes doesn't, politely ask them to send only items they know or suspect are relevant to you. If their information is of limited or no utility, stop receiving it by unsubscribing, or by creating a Rule to move their messages directly to your Deleted Items (in Microsoft Outlook, right-click on an e-mail and go to Create Rule and check the appropriate boxes). Those rare nuggets of useful information just aren't worth the

---

⊕ If it takes you more than a minute to find a file, document, or e-mail, something's wrong. Develop a more efficient information processing/filing system.

🕐 Do you really need to receive the jokes and lists
your coworkers circulate? Just reading them wastes your
time, so politely ask your colleagues to stop sending
them to you, or give them a personal e-mail address.

time you'll spend sorting through the mountain of garbage. You're better off doing your own search for the information when you need it.

For all other unwanted mail, put the address of the sender on your Junk or "blacklist," so you never have to see the e-mail (in Outlook, right-click on an e-mail, select Junk e-mail, and add them to your blocked senders list). That way, when you receive a new e-mail message from that person, it will go to your Junk mail folder, where you can review it before you delete it, to ensure something important didn't get filtered out, which can happen occasionally.

Some find it easier to set up a "whitelist." Whereas a blacklist specifies the addresses you refuse to receive e-mails from, a whitelist contains only the addresses you're *willing* to receive e-mail from. You can easily arrange an autoresponder to deal with people outside your immediate circle who need to get in touch with you, simply by directing them to call you. Or you can use a Challenge Response E-mail service such as Spam Arrest. At the very least, delete the obvious junk without opening it. Just by looking at the return address and subject line, you can tell which e-mails are important and which ones aren't.

Research Effectively

It pays to hone your research skills. For example: If you learn how to use online search engines more effectively, you won't spend so much time in fruitless searching. Be very specific about what you're looking for. Most search engines use a standardized set of "Boolean operators" (plus and minus signs;

quotation marks; and words like AND, OR, and NOT, etc.) to help you link keywords more effectively and thus weed out most useless search results. Thus, "Mexican-American War" +Texas -"Zachary Taylor" will return a somewhat different set of results than typing Mexican-American War without quotation marks.

Similarly, if you Google the words "save time," you might get 241,000,000 responses. Among the top ten you might have images of clocks, a Wikipedia article on daylight savings time, an organization selling posters for the workplace on saving time, a PDF of Microsoft Office keyboard shortcuts, and several articles offering time-saving tips from authors like Yours Truly. They all have their place, but may not be what you're looking for at that moment. When you add a few words to your search, making it "how to save time," you eliminate the clock images, the Wikipedia article, and the posters, trimming the list down to 148,000,000 responses—with the top ten all being articles about time-savings tricks and ideas. Or add the words 'picture' or 'video' or 'lyrics' in front of your search. The Advanced Search feature in Google provides a self-explanatory way to narrow your search results.

As you can see, effective researching starts with knowing the right questions to ask, no matter what tools you select for the job. Do it *before* you go searching for the answers. Here's a more complex example. Let's say you have to make a recommendation to a university about buying PC or Mac computers for a particular lab. Before you start, decide what criteria would affect your recommendation. Among the many questions you might ask are:

- How much does each computer cost?
- Which platform do professionals in the relevant field use most?
- Which platform has better software availability?
- Which platform has fewer maintenance problems?

- How much training will be necessary if we switch or upgrade?

Those questions provide a starting point for your research. Without them, your research is undirected, and may produce equivocal results. Additionally, you'll waste a lot of time reviewing material that doesn't affect your recommendation.

You can also leverage library services to limit your research time. Libraries are largely digitized these days, but many still offer valuable resources beyond the online catalog to those willing to learn about and use them. Most librarians are happy to show you various tips, tricks, and shortcuts to minimize time spent searching for information, and there are special services available to help you hunt down and borrow obscure sources.

If you can't spare the time at all, consider delegating some of your research. Either hire specialized researchers to do the job, or, if it's within your power, assign the work to others in your organization. If you delegate research to more than one person, assign different, distinct topics to each person, to limit wasteful overlap.

🕐 Not everything has been digitized yet, so if your library lacks a particular resource you need, ask the librarian to arrange an interlibrary loan.

Maximize Your Reading Time

Because we're visual beings, reading remains one of the best ways to absorb copious amounts of information rapidly. Depending on your job, you may find it necessary to add reading periods to your schedule or spend the occasional weekend catching up. In addition, carry reading material with you at all

🕐 If you'd rather not carry around a bundle of papers
for downtime reading, consider carrying an e-reader
or small tablet computer. You can easily scan and
convert paper files to electronic formats, and most
tablets have apps that let you mark them up, too.

times. That way, you can use unscheduled downtime to absorb new information.

As for the reading itself, I recommend the Rhythmic Perusal method, developed by the University of Minnesota's J. Michael Bennett. With this method, you first focus on the purpose and title (or subtitle) of what you're reading. Relax your face. Scan the upper surfaces of the words in a line, reading the entire line in a single smooth movement. Look for particularly meaningful phrases and terms, and read more for thoughts, feelings, and ideas than the words themselves.

Integrate Your New Information

Once you've internalized new information, put your subconscious mind to work. Most creative ideas come when you're not trying to think of a solution. Ideas often come to me in the middle of the night or on a stroll. It's as though my brain is "working on it" behind the scenes, and answers suddenly pop into my head. Many others tell me they get their best ideas when not deliberately thinking about an issue. Let any problems presented by new information percolate in the back of your mind for a while, or use a mind map or other brainstorming tool.

When your mind does solve something, it may present you with those new ideas, associations, and connections unexpectedly. Don't forget to capture new thoughts and ideas immediately. Ideas are like slippery fish: You have to hook them with some easy-to-carry recording method, or they'll get away. Where do you put all those great ideas?

🕐 If you lack pen and paper to hook a slippery idea
with, leave a voicemail on your work phone.

FILING PRECEPTS

Look at your desk right now. Are there piles of paper everywhere? If you're like 90 percent of office workers, the answer is a resounding "Yes!" So, whatever happened to the paperless office all the business gurus promised us? We're getting better, but clearly it hasn't come to pass quite yet. So we still need places to put all our paper.

If you're swamped with paper, then you're in dire need of an effective filing system. Personal filing and time management systems are very personal decisions; my needs may be different from yours, so tailor this system to your requirements.

Here are the categories I recommend considering for your filing system.

- *Active/Dynamic files.* Accessed daily. A tickler file (see below) is a prime example of this category.
- *Project/Client files.* Accessed at least once a month. These may include meeting notes, committee paperwork, newsletters you write, etc.
- *Reference files.* Accessed at least once a year. For example, completed project files, tax paperwork, personnel information, and budgets.
- *Archive/History files.* Accessed less than once a year. Store these somewhere clean, dry, and away from your office.

While these are the standard categories, you can also add any others you find useful: for example, Product Sheets, Topi-

---

🕑 Don't create just a paper-based filing system.
Develop a logical system for your electronic files as well,
using folders and easily remembered naming conventions.

---

cal Information, Research, Ideas, etc. Again, whatever works best for you is fine. Just use an easily-remembered noun as the first word in each file title; use subcategories to better organize your files; add information in a consistent manner; and, most important of all, file your paperwork a few times a month at the minimum! You can't afford to have your files pile up until they're a mile high.

The Tickler File

In my opinion, the tickler file is among the most important components of any paper filing system; it allows you to retrieve specific items related to a specific day. For example, if you receive a meeting request via e-mail and accept it, the appointment moves to your calendar for you. But the invitation might have an attachment you wish to print and take to the meeting with you. That hardcopy piece of paper would be filed in your Tickler file, in the folder corresponding to the day of the meeting. Outlook maintains your calendar digitally; however, it can't hold a physical piece of paper.

Think of a Tickler as a rotating annual calendar for paper. To set one up, start with forty-three hanging folders (Pendaflex style, not file folders): thirty-one folders for the days of the month and twelve for the months. Hang your folders somewhere very convenient; a desk drawer is your best option, or you can set up a rolling file or a rack on your desk. Anywhere is fine, as long as you don't have to get up to reach it.

Arrange it so when you open the drawer, the first folder you see is the folder for the current month. Hanging behind it is the folder with the number of today's date, followed by the folder for tomorrow, and so on through the days. The rest of the months hang behind it. In your drawer, it might look something like this:

March
      15
      16 . . .
      31
April
      1
      2 . . .
      14
May . . .
February

Next, file all the papers requiring some future action. Let's say you receive an invoice due on the 14th of a particular month. You wouldn't want to file this in the 14 folder, because the payment would arrive late. File things on the day you need to see them again. You might file the invoice in the 7 folder, so it comes up soon enough for you to pay it before it's due. Always ask yourself, "When do I need to see this again?"

Each evening, pull the next day's file, preferably as the last action before you leave the office. Hence, if today is the 28th, before leaving for the day, pull the contents of the file marked 29. The agenda for tomorrow's meeting will appear as if by magic! Then move that folder behind the 28th of the following month. So dated folders move to the next month, and monthly folders move to the back of the drawer.

🕐 You can still use the tickler file concept even when trying to go paperless. Use your e-mail tools to create reminders on Sent Items or set Start and Due dates in Tasks.

YOUR PERSONAL TIME MANAGEMENT SYSTEM

You'll also want to track all the basic information required to keep your life and schedule moving along smoothly. To a large extent, this will depend on the personal time management system you adopt—paper-based, electronic, or some hybrid method of both.

Personal information arrives and gets stored in myriad ways today, due to all of the shiny new technologies available in our world. Most people track contacts, communication, meetings and appointments, Master lists, HIT (daily) lists, and notes within their personal systems. Today, your system could include:

- Information-capturing methods, including software such as Evernote or Microsoft OneNote, or paper methods such as a Day-Timer or notebook
- Customer relationship management (CRM) software, such as ACT, GoldMine, or Salesforce.com
- Social media channels, each with its own inbox, such as LinkedIn, Twitter, Facebook, YouTube, or Foursquare
- Information delivery software such as e-mail, intranets, and instant messages
- Texting and apps using your favorite smartphone or hand-held (e.g., iPad), such as Plan2Go by Day-Timer
- Web services to help you stay organized, such as Nozbe by Michael Sliwinski, or Remember the Milk

Obviously, there's no single "correct" method here. Your personal time management system will evolve over time to fit your requirements. The challenge is that effective time management actually involves three separate functions:

1. *Capture* inputs as they occur to you or are received.
2. *Organize* the information into tasks and start/due dates.
3. *Reference* what you need to do.

Many people use one tool for all three functions; however, three different methods might actually be more effective for some people. Some people are trying to go "paperless" and use a handheld that syncs to their e-mail and calendar, which is just fine, and they enter new tasks directly into their handheld. But if you're a "paper" person, this might not work well for you. If you think of something to do, your first instinct might be to grab a piece of paper and a pencil, not your phone. So, you could use paper for your capture method and the phone for your reference tool, and that would be perfectly organized as well.

For example, I love my handheld but hate tapping tasks into it. When I think of something to do, my instant reaction is to grab a pencil and write in my Master or HIT list in my Day-Timer. Anything left over at the end of the day gets entered into my Task list in Outlook. My phone syncs up and then acts as a reference tool for contacts, calendar, e-mail, and tasks, so I can scan it at any time, even when I'm not in front of my computer.

So my time management system looks like this:

1. *Capture:* Productivity Pro® Day-Timer
2. *Organize:* Outlook Tasks
3. *Reference:* Droid handheld

What's yours? Other people capture on their iPad, which is just great, if you are willing to do that consistently, every single time you think of something to do, and not just "some" times. What if you're on a plane, with all your electronic devices off, or in a meeting, where it appears you are texting if you type yourself a note? Personally, I find entering tasks into my handheld tedious (the buttons are small and I hate typos). Needless to say, some methods work better than others.

You Look Like You Need a HUG!

Regardless of the time management system you choose to organize your life, there are a few foundational principles for maximizing any system's efficiency. I call these the "HUG" criteria.

H—Handy. Is your system available at all times, or are you what I call a "scrapper"? Scrappers are easily identifiable by all the little scraps of paper everywhere. What happens when you go to a restaurant to meet with a friend or client, and you need to write something down, and you don't have anything to write on? What do you grab—a napkin? A dry cleaning receipt? An envelope? The back of a business card? Have you ever written on your hand in desperation? (I call this the original PalmPilot®). Well, if you're a scrapper, it's simple to fix. Whether you're using a handheld, iPad, notebook, or the Productivity Pro® Day-Timer, carry your system with you at all times. It *must* be available, because scheduling meetings or checking due dates can happen in the oddest of places. If your system is too cumbersome to keep with you all the time, then you'll want to switch to something more portable—something more "Handy."

🕑 A contact file should include the person's company, main office phone number, cell phone number, e-mail address, personal office number/extension, and physical address.

U—Usable. To be truly usable, your personal time management system must bring together the personal and professional aspects of your life in one place, making it easy to switch between them. Everything needs to be included: calendars, to-do lists, work schedules, private schedules, family schedules, kid activities, personal appointments, vacation plans, professional and private contacts—the works. In particular, all your calendars should be included (such as syncing your Google calendar to your work calendar on your phone); otherwise, conflicts are inevitable. For example: If you can't check to see if your son has soccer practice on Thursday afternoon, because you've left your family calendar at home or on the refrigerator, then you might inadvertently plan a business meeting at the same time—and end up with a conflict. It's better and easier to keep your entire life in one place, in a format you can easily reference at all times.

G—Garbage-free. If you use a planner, binder, or notebook, what would happen if you picked it up and shook it? Would you witness a blizzard of falling papers? Any loose papers you're working with should go in a file folder or your briefcase. Remember to reduce, reduce, and reduce again! Trim your system down to the categories you intend to use. Just because you have apps on your phone or an extra tab in your planner doesn't mean you actually have to use them. Move, remove, or convert them to some other use. Even handheld users who don't use them consistently end up with scraps of paper everywhere.

The System of Your Dreams

Does your time management system meet the HUG criteria? No? Keep tweaking it until you discover your best fit! If it does cover these three bases and it works for you, then you have the right personal time management system in place. If it frustrates you in some way, continue to make adjustments. Don't feel pressured to move to a particular system if it's a poor fit to your personality, or isn't suited to your work and life situation. I've known people who were entirely paperless who went back to paper to a limited extent, because they discovered they were more organized with paper than without it.

🕐 Test your personal time management system for HUGability. It needs to be Handy, Usable, and Garbage-free.

BASIC INFORMATION HANDLING

In just about any office job, you encounter a constant flood of new information. You have no choice but to take it all in and process it one way or another—lest you drown in it. Some of this information will come to you automatically; some you'll have to dig up yourself. However we acquire it, we all must filter, process, think about, focus on, reference, and internalize the information, incorporating it into our organizational systems, processes, and daily routine as appropriate.

As you do so, keep these six simple rules in mind:

1. *The Superglue Rule.* The very first time you touch an item, pretend it's stuck to your hand (as in paper) or your eyes (as in e-mail) or your ear (as in voicemail). You can't put it down until you've made a decision (next step).

2. *The Decisiveness Rule.* Decide right away what to do with the item. Any decision is better than no decision. Indecision actually causes clutter! Luckily, there are only six potential decisions, which I'll outline in the upcoming 6-D System.

3. *The Start-to-Finish Rule.* Don't just decide what to do with an item—do it! This doesn't necessarily mean you'll complete the item, because doing it later is actually a decision. Every decision has an "end" point, so make sure you don't stop it halfway through the process. Incompletions are very stressful (ever had a "half-organized" closet?).

4. *The Three-Minute Rule.* If you can easily process a piece of information in three minutes or less, get it done right then and off your plate before moving to the next item.

5. *The Empty Inbox Rule.* Don't use your inbox as a to-do list or filing system. Once you get past a screen shot or so, you have to start scrolling and re-reading. You must pull the action out of each item, or you'll have random due dates mixed together and won't know when to begin what. Instead, process every single piece of incoming information

and get it out of the inbox and into the right location (more on this to come).

6. *The Discipline Rule.* Spend a few minutes handling and organizing your new information every day. Then you won't have to stay late or come in on a Saturday just to clean up your backlog.

Clearly, some of these rules are interrelated, and how you use one is likely to influence how you use others. Now you have a simple set of principles to guide your actions, so let's take a look at handling the flow of incoming information.

THE 6-D INFORMATION MANAGEMENT SYSTEM™

I've taught my 6-D Information Management System since the 1990s (lots of people have created takeoffs on this system). I call it the 6-D System because it's based on six decisions, all beginning with the letter "D." You can use the system to process and fine-tune *any* type of information. In this section, we'll first review the general meaning for each "D," and then we'll apply the decisions to the three most common media in the modern workplace: paper, e-mail, and voicemail.

Six Basic Decisions

1. *Discard.* I've put this decision first, because whatever you don't get rid of, you'll have to work through your system. You'll benefit from getting rid of as much as possible at the outset. Don't think, "I might need this again someday." Instead, ask yourself, "Why should I keep this?" Have a good reason to keep something. Otherwise, take a deep breath and toss it!

2. *Delegate.* If you can't throw something away, perhaps you can give it away to someone else. This doesn't always mean delegation in a formal sense, if the person doesn't work for you. In fact, you may actually be the one to whom work is delegated. So sometimes you could "Discuss" the issue

(that might be another good "D" here), or you could "Distribute" it. The goal is to transfer it from your sphere of control to someone else's.

3. *Do.* The item requires your personal action, and you can handle it right then.

4. *Date.* There's future action required, but you can't do it now. Some people have tried to use the words "Delay" or "Defer" in this instance, but I caution against doing so, because those terms don't specify how long you're delaying it. (This would be like having a giant folder called "Pending" or "Waiting on.") Instead of continually scanning a list or pile over and over again, be specific with this step and assign a date you need to see, think about, or otherwise handle the item again.

5. *Drawer.* These items need to be filed in a drawer for future reference. No action is required, but you can't toss it either. You might want to access it again just in case, so you should save it.

6. *Deter.* Stop the information from ever coming across your desk or landing in one of your inboxes again. You're not merely throwing it away; you're making sure you've eliminated the possibility it will come back to you. You may have to take some extra steps to make sure you stop these items in their tracks.

And that's it! Those are the six decisions you use to process any piece of information. Now, let's review the equivalent action steps and apply the 6 Ds to the three primary types of information entering your system: paper, e-mail, and voicemail.

⊕ Although I've designed the 6-D System specifically for handling information, you can also apply the general concepts more broadly to task triage, per Chapter 1.

Paper Equivalents

Let's discuss applying each decision to a hardcopy piece of paper (regular mail, interoffice mail, printed Internet information, printed e-mail, etc.). Referring to the Ds above, the equivalent action steps would be:

1. Throw it away, recycle it, or shred confidential documents. You're done! You followed the Start-to-Finish Rule: You reviewed it, made a decision, and took action.

2. Get the paper into the hands of another person. What are the options for doing this? If you're both in the same building, you might route it to them through interoffice mail or hand-deliver it. For people located elsewhere, you could scan and e-mail the paper, or fax it as appropriate. You might also snail-mail or FedEx it to them. Remember the Superglue Rule: While it's in your hand, consider it stuck to you. You can't un-stick it until you make a decision about what to do it with it. Then once you decide to send it to someone else, don't put it down and go on to the next thing until it's in an "Out" box. Whatever it takes, make sure each piece has moved through your system before going on to the next item.

3. If you can't throw away the paper or give it to someone else, go ahead and Do it. The very next question you have to ask yourself is, "Can I do this in three minutes or less?" If the answer is yes, then, per the Three-Minute Rule, respond to the request right away (check this box, sign here, comment here, review this, etc.). Move small tasks out of your office immediately before they accumulate. It's more efficient to do these immediately than to put them down and have to pick them up and reread them again. Get used to completing quick things without delay.

4. If you can't do it now, ask yourself, "When do I need to see this again?" and file it in the appropriate Tickler file folder, where it will magically pop up again on that date.

5. Integrate reference papers into your regular filing system. If it doesn't require any action, put it in a "to be filed" bin or immediately file it in the appropriate physical file (client, project, reference, idea, subject, etc.) if you prefer.

6. To prevent a piece of paper from coming back again, you have to remove yourself from the distribution list. Unsubscribe or, as appropriate, tell the person sending you the item you're no longer on the team or committee, and therefore don't need to receive that information anymore. If you receive mail for someone who's no longer there, just write on the outside "No longer here" and put it in the outbound mail.

Voicemail Equivalents

Now let's apply the same Ds to a voicemail message on your office or cell phone. Many people listening to voicemail hit "Save" too often—and soon they have many, many saved voicemails. Instead, process the voicemail through the 6-D system. The very first time you listen to it, it's stuck to your ear, so focus on making a decision to get it out of your voicemail inbox.

1. Once you've listened to the voicemail, just delete it.

2. Forward the voicemail to another person and ask that person to respond. If you're expecting an answer, make sure to indicate in your time management system you left the person a message. I tag my calls on my HIT list with an "M" if I left a message. In your weekly review, you'll see who didn't get back to you with an answer. You can also do this with a Reminder on an Outlook Task.

3. If you can respond right away, leave an answer in that person's voicemail or call them back.

4. If you need to call someone back but can't do it immediately, don't just hit Save! To date a voicemail, you could write a note and phone number on your HIT list and delete the voicemail. You could create an electronic Task.

You might type the message into your CRM database and schedule a return call. You might flag the person in your Contacts with a reminder set for when to call back. You might have a spiral notebook you use just for phone calls. You could write a note and file it in your Tickler file. You might type into an iPad or Droid app. Anything is better than using sticky notes! The point is to get the message off your voicemail and decide on a consistent method for recording calls in one place.

5. If someone leaves you information on your voicemail that you need to save, don't just save the message. Instead, transcribe it, enter it in your CRM, or create a Journal entry in Outlook, tagged to the correct Contact. Bottom line: Get it off the voicemail and into your trusted retrieval method for historical communications.

6. How do you keep people from leaving you voicemails? I like to change my outgoing greeting when I'm out of the office to something like, "I'm not in the office right now. For immediate assistance . . ." and then give them a way to get out of the voicemail system, such as hitting o and dialing 2 to be transferred to another person. Or I suggest they e-mail instead. People want to have good service even when you're not there. Some may still leave voicemails, but you'll receive fewer than you would have with a standard out-of-office message.

E-mail Equivalents

Undoubtedly, your e-mail is probably the biggest organizational challenge you deal with today. Make no mistake: E-mail actually *is* your work, because all those messages represent something you need to do and decisions you need to make. But many people are paralyzed by the sheer volume of messages or don't have a systematic way of pulling action from e-mail. So most people leave messages in their inboxes to languish and get buried by the onslaught of new incoming e-mails.

I'm a Microsoft Certified Application Specialist in Outlook (MCAS), and I've been providing Outlook training to
corporate clients (including Microsoft!) since the 1990s.[20]
I believe there's no better tool than Outlook for managing
and integrating your e-mail, tasks, notes, contacts, journal,
and calendar. But many people simply don't know how to
get the most out of Outlook, because it's not the most user-
friendly piece of software. I'd estimate most people use about
15–25 percent of its capabilities. Most training consists of
"here's your inbox; have fun." So in this section, I'll explain
the processes of using Microsoft Outlook, since around 95
percent of my corporate clients use this software. A few others use Lotus Notes, GroupWise, Google Mail, Outlook for
Mac, or Mac Mail. The principles are exactly the same, but
you'll need to figure out the commands for your particular
platform.

Let's walk through e-mail processing using my 6-D
System:

1. Delete the e-mail. It's the simplest and most effective way
to reduce your e-mail volume. This doesn't require extensive explanation; I hope use your delete key often—about
80 percent of the time!

2. Forward it to someone else and either delete or file the
original e-mail so it's no longer in your Inbox. Or send
a Task Request (right-click, select Move to Folder, select
Tasks, click the Assign Task button, type in the person's
name, type instructions, and Send.) The e-mail is gone
from your Inbox but can be seen in Tasks when you View
by Person Responsible. Now you'll easily see who owes
you what.

3. If you can't delete or forward an e-mail, and it's a simple
e-mail requiring a quick answer, follow the Three-Minute
Rule. Just hit Reply, type, send, delete/file, and move to
the next. Get it out of that inbox! Stop clicking around and
reading e-mail without replying to it.

4. The fourth step, Date, is the big black hole of e-mail management. If an e-mail requires a reply but you can't do it now, what should you do with it? Do not leave it in your inbox! You also don't want to simply file it (unless you made a task or a note), because you might forget about it. How do you ensure you'll see that e-mail again on a specific day, such that you have time to handle it before it's due? That's the big question. You need the electronic equivalent of the paper tickler file, so you're seeing only the e-mails you need to see, on the day you need to see them. More information for dating e-mails is given below.

5. File the e-mail in a personal folder. Alternatively, some people like to do a File, Save As, and save the e-mail as an .msg file (Outlook message format) on a hard or shared drive (in the same way you would a Word document or PowerPoint deck).

6. Unsubscribe, create a Rule, or add the sender to the blocked senders list. If you change your mind, you can always select "Not Junk" to trust e-mail from that source, and it will move it back into your Inbox.

So let's discuss some different options for Step 4, dating an e-mail. You have several choices.

Convert the e-mail to a Task.[21] In Outlook, you can right-click on a message and choose the option to "Move to Folder." Or, if you opened the e-mail, look for the "Move to Folder" button. Or, if you're an icon person, it's the one that looks like a piece of paper with an arrow into a folder. Personally, I like to right-click, as this presents me with a context-sensitive menu. Outlook presents you with a dialog box, asking which folder you'd like to move the item into. If it's something you need to *do*, select Tasks. If it's connected to a specific *time*, for example a lunch date, then select Calendar. Don't put things you need to do in your calendar, because if you don't get it done, you have to manually change the date to another day. Tasks, however, roll forward automatically. A new Task or Appointment will be automatically created, and your e-mail with attachments will be included in the text portion. In the Task, fill in the Start Date, which is the date you want to *see* the item again. The Due Date is when you must *complete* the item. Set a Start Date, because if something is due on the 30th, it won't help you to see it on the 30th if it will take several days to complete it. You need to see it when you have to *begin* the task. Unfortunately, Outlook is set to have the To-Do bar display the "Today" flag by Due Date, so you have to change it to arrange by "Start Date." It doesn't matter when it's due; it matters only that you see it again in enough time to complete it before it's due!

Note: It's important to use the "Move to Folder" command (and select Tasks or Calendar) rather than just dragging and dropping an e-mail. If you just drag an e-mail to Tasks, it will create a *copy* of the e-mail from your Inbox, and the attachments don't go with it. Later, you'd have to waste time locating it so you can respond to the original e-mail. Using the "Move to Folder, Tasks" feature, you can open the e-mail from inside the Task itself and reply. You have to get out of the mindset that an e-mail has to be in the inbox in order to reply to it.

Print the e-mail and file in your tickler file. Some people are still paper people and like to print e-mails. If you must print yours, file it in your paper tickler file, and move the e-mail to a personal folder called "@Tickler," so you know where to locate it when it comes up in your tickler file. That way, your Inbox contains unprocessed work, and your @Tickler contains only processed work, triggered by date in your Tickler.

Create reminders from Sent Items. Perhaps you want to receive a reminder on an e-mail you sent, to confirm that your request was completed, or that you received the answer you needed, etc. Click on your Sent Items and find the message you just sent. Drag that e-mail to Tasks (thus creating a copy, so it doesn't move out of your Sent Items). Click the Reminder box and set a date you expect to hear back. (Don't set a Start Date or Due Date, so it doesn't show up in your To-Do bar.) When you get the Reminder pop-up box, you can open each one and review. If you received a reply, mark it complete or delete it. If you haven't heard back, you can forward or re-send your original e-mail to follow up.

Flag an e-mail. I don't prefer this method, because if you flag an item in your inbox, you are *not* creating a Task; you're creating a To-Do. Yes, it shows up in your To-Do list, but the original stays in your inbox (unlike the "Right-click, Move to Folder, Tasks" option I discussed earlier). An exception is Outlook version 2010, where you can now right-click on the flag, choose add a Reminder (this is the same reminder box that pops up right before a meeting), select the date you need to see it again, and then move it to any personal folder. In 2010, the reminder will now go off regardless of what folder it's located in. I simply prefer to convert mine to Tasks. It's not right or wrong; it's just personal preference.

Use the Search Folders to find items for follow up. Let's say you set a flag to notify you just in case you don't hear back from a certain person by October 6 at noon. Once you have a reminder set, you can move the e-mail into a personal folder. If you're not in Outlook 2010, you can click on the "+" next to your Search Folders (at the bottom of the Navigation pane), and choose "For Follow Up." Voilà—there are all the e-mails you've flagged or set a reminder on. With this method, you don't have to sort your flag column to search for e-mails.

THE E-MAIL DECISION TREE

In summary, a single e-mail could actually require you to:

1. *Read the e-mail.*
2. *Make a decision* (refer to the 6 Ds above).
3. *Complete the appropriate action:*
    A. *Can you handle it immediately?* Options:
        1. Delete.
        2. Forward.
        3. Send as a Task Request.
        4. Reply with an answer and delete or file.
        5. Reply to acknowledge receipt and give a promised deadline.
    B. *Do you need to work it later* (or decide later)?
        6. In Outlook, select "Move to Folder," Task (for to-do items); fill in Start and Due Dates for HIT list. Or set a Reminder and use the Reminder dialog box as a mini to-do list.
        7. In Outlook, select "Move to Folder," Calendar (for appointments), fill in day/time.
    C. *Does it require no action, but you need to save it?* Options:
        8. Be the last one to reply and delete. Use your Sent Items for filing.
        9. Save the e-mail in your personal folders.
        10. File, Save as .msg file on hard drive or shared drive.
    D. *Can you keep it from coming again?* Options:
        11. Unsubscribe.
        12. Add Sender to Junk list.
        13. Create a Rule to move to Deleted Items.
4. *Schedule any follow-up.* Set follow-up reminders for pending action or promised deliverables. Drag the Sent Item to Tasks and set a Reminder.
5. *On the designated Start Date, complete the required task.*
    - What is the end result?
    - Who needs to be involved?

- Who should own it?
- What steps are required?
- Respond with the requested information.
  6. *Store the supporting information.*

Bottom Line: Always 6-D Everything!

When handling information, remember these 6 Ds: Discard, Delegate, Do, Date, Drawer, or Deter. Every time you touch a new piece of paper, open a new e-mail, or get a new voicemail, force yourself to choose one of the 6 Ds.

If you have hundreds or thousands of e-mails in your inbox, create a new folder called "old inbox." Drag all your e-mails into it. Practice keeping your inbox empty with all new e-mails coming in. Thirty minutes each day, 6-D your old e-mail, until your "old inbox" folder and inbox are both finally empty.

Yes, implementing the 6-D formula will require an additional level of time investment initially. However, once you've formed a new habit and have cleaned up your inbox, you'll save a nice little chunk of time each day that can go toward your ninety-minute total.

Avoid the Fatal Flaw

Spotting incompetence is simple. Look for people who know full well what they need to change to become more productive but refuse to do so. You know the one. "Yeah, I know I need to organize my files, but that's just how I am. Always been this way. You should see my clothes closet at home."

Gee, now there's something to broadcast!

When employees telegraph their areas of inefficiency, almost as if to brag about their bad habits, you know you're dealing with someone who will most likely never "get" the productivity message.

We all have flaws and areas in need of improvement—a normal and healthy condition. Moreover, sometimes these weaknesses remain in our blind spots for a time. But the moment your awareness has been raised—either by introspection or by another person—you have an obligation to begin remedying the productivity flaw, not celebrating it. Those who celebrate inefficiency, in information processing or anything else, single themselves out as incompetent.

SUMMARY: PWF STEP 4 CHECKUP

Modern office workers face an astonishing flood of information, flowing in from more sources than we've ever before experienced. If you can't learn how to filter out the worthless and efficiently organize the remainder, your productivity will inevitably suffer.

First, establish a basic filing system to track your paper documents, including the following types of files at the very least: Active/Dynamic, Project/Client, Reference, and Archive/History. Next, set up a personal time management system, if you haven't already. It doesn't matter whether you choose a paper-based, electronic, or hybrid method, as long as it meets the HUG criteria: it must be Handy, Usable, and Garbage-free. Having these systems in place will help you tame the information glut.

Next, find ways to reduce the involuntary data inflow, especially via e-mail. If possible, have someone else sort through it for you. Otherwise, stop receiving information you don't need, and set up spam filters, blacklists, whitelists, and rules to automatically delete e-mail.

When voluntarily taking in information, winnow it down using the appropriate research techniques, especially when searching the Internet. In addition, leverage any available library services to cut down your research time and maximize your results.

Carry reading material with you constantly, so you can make effective use of unscheduled downtime, and investigate speed-reading techniques that let you get the most out of the reading time you do have.

Basic information handling skills are also critical:

- Don't touch things multiple times.
- Be decisive and apply the basic precepts of my 6-D Information Handling System—Discard, Delegate, Do, Date, Drawer, or Deter.
- Start what you finish.
- Do things right away if they require less than three minutes.
- Don't use your inboxes as a to-do list.
- Empty your inboxes at least once daily.

Apply these rules to all incoming information, particularly paper, e-mail, and voicemail.

5

Close the Loop

The fifth step in the Productivity Workflow Formula involves consolidating everything you've established in the previous steps, ensuring that the various components work together smoothly, feeding back the results, and making the entire process flow more efficiently. You've been building a foundation for a more efficient lifestyle by reducing your to-do list, calendar commitments, distractions, and incoming information.

Closing the loop means you're constantly paying attention to and communicating about hitting goals, meeting deadlines, fulfilling promises, and committing to teamwork. Status changes can occur by the minute, so as you get new information, constantly weed out the unnecessary.

As part of the process, you will re-connect with your leadership and your teams, reaffirm your important tasks, and verify your strategic direction. There's also a continuous improvement component: When a process seems unusually long and inefficient, do what you can to make it easier for everyone. Just because something's been done a certain way for a long time doesn't mean it's the best way to do it now. If you find a problem, fix it if you can, or offer a solution if you can't.

🕐 Don't change for the sake of change. If an
existing system works well and you can't think of a
better way to do it, then why fix it or upgrade it?

ORGANIZED IMPLEMENTATION

A high level of organization leaves little, if anything, to chance. In addition to increasing efficiency, you'll appear more professional when organized. You'll impress your clients with your ability to easily find files, details, and paperwork. Conversely, clients will be disturbed if you're unable to quickly access the information you need. With a great system in place, you'll look more professional and will quickly serve the needs of your clients, coworkers, and employer.

Here are a few starting points you can implement fairly quickly, as you put more long-term processes into place:

- Get rid of clutter. It's distracting, and makes it harder to find things.
- Organize your entire workspace for maximum efficiency, eliminating any frustrations.
- Purge computer and paper files to make more room and simplify organization.
- Implement simple but logical filing and naming conventions for your computer files.
- Tweak your logistics and prepare resources in advance of your anticipated needs.
- Set up shortcuts for all standard tasks.
- Automate tasks or processes you'll do more than twice.

In the grander scheme of things, you'll want to define long-term organizational and procedural goals, and then proactively decide the best ways to move toward them. Be specific, whatever it means to you in terms of time, money, numbers, or any other metric.

Creating a detailed organizational plan of action is essential not just to bringing everything together, but to implementing it all and maintaining your personal momentum. This isn't really something you can do on the fly; make time to sit down and plan out the details, or your attempts are likely to fail. Plan the various aspects of your system, integrate them, understand the details of how they fit together—and then confidently execute your solutions. Once they're in play, make every effort to keep the loop tightly closed. This will require constant attention to detail, and immediate action to fix or replace the things that are not working well.

🕐 Learn the keyboard shortcuts for all your computer programs, and program macros for common tasks. You'll save a surprising amount of time.

THE PEOPLE PROBLEM

People will inevitably cause breakdowns in your workflow loop. We try to do our best, but we make mistakes, we forget, we let deadlines slip, we communicate poorly, we suffer illness and injury—and as a result of all this, we inadvertently damage our own and other people's productivity. Here are some people issues to look out for and suggestions on handling them.

Closing Communication Loops

One factor that sets human beings apart from the rest of creation is our ability to communicate in great detail, with a minimum of confusion and unproductive "noise." Still, it's amazing how easy it is to *fail* to communicate properly. The annals of history are replete with episodes of poor communication (or a complete lack thereof), leading to widespread misery and pain. On a lesser scale, individuals and businesses have to deal with miscommunication issues every single day; in the workplace, such issues can have a severe impact not just on individual productivity, but on the overall bottom line.

Even minor corporate miscommunications can prove costly. Here's an interesting example. Once I worked with the president of an automotive parts manufacturing organization, who called someone in finance to get a figure to put into a speech he was planning. The president expected him to spend maybe fifteen minutes on a rough estimate. Instead, the finance guy spent *ten* hours coming up with an exact figure. It turned out all the president was looking for was a high-level guess—was it $5 million, or $50 million?

Whose fault was this miscommunication? It was both their faults. The president should have said, "I'm looking for this type of number, and I'm thinking it'll just take you fifteen minutes or so to ballpark it, plus or minus a few million dollars. Does that sound reasonable?" The finance person could have said, "To get you the figure you're requesting, it's going to take me this much time—is that what you want?" The president could have then decided whether or not it was worth the effort.

Clearly, then, your ability to communicate is a critical productivity tool, especially in terms of how you word your communications, and your level of aggressiveness in expressing your needs and requirements. Even when the lines of communication are wide open, beating around the bush, couching your message in obscure terms, or burying it in a mass of unnecessary verbiage may cause mental static in the people with whom you're trying to communicate, resulting in confusion and irritation. At best, this will slow them down; at worst, they may ignore you. Either outcome will damage productivity, both yours and theirs.

Therefore, whether you're communicating with employees

or superiors, make every effort to get your point across with a minimum of noise. Choose your words with great care, saying precisely what you mean, as directly as possible. Let's consider several ways you can do this.

Get straight to the point. Have you ever tried to talk to someone who rambled, refused to give a straight answer, or danced around the subject? If you have, then you know how annoying and nonproductive it can be. Perhaps the person was afraid you'd get angry if he came right out and said what he wanted to say; maybe he wanted attention; or maybe he just liked to hear himself speak.

The reason why doesn't matter. It doesn't even matter if the person was amusing or instructive to listen to, as ramblers sometimes are. What matters is that they wasted your time, and their own, by not getting straight to the point. You don't want to do this to other people, so make your communications concise.

Some people avoid brevity because they don't want to seem rude; admittedly, verbal interaction is useful in the workplace as a form of social lubrication. There's no doubt politeness pays, and playing nice will help you stay in your coworkers' good graces. Nonetheless, in most workplace situations, you'll want to be direct. You can smile when you do so, to take the edge off for the easily offended.

If you have a hard time with straightforward communication, practice what you want to say in advance. Take a results-oriented stance, envisioning exactly what you want to achieve. Then edit your message toward that end to make it plain and specific. Tweak your message to avoid sounding brusque, and then deliver it assertively, as simply as possible.

Avoid unnecessary qualifiers and hedging. Some people just can't seem to deliver any message, especially a request, firmly and directly. They hem in everything they say with so many

qualifiers—"what if's," "maybe's," and "could be's"—that ultimately what they're trying to say gets lost, causing the recipi-
ents to waste time on interpretation and clarification.

In other cases, the bad communicator hedges the message
to make it seem less important than it actually is. Instead of
just telling the IT Department that they need a certain backup
file right away, for example, they might say something like,
"Um, if you have a chance, could you pull this file for me? No
hurry." The recipient may now ignore the request or push it
down the priority scale, because the sender hasn't made the
urgency clear.

My roots are German on my father's side, and we have a
word for this kind of poor communication: "mealy-mouthed,"
from the old German slang term for an inability to communicate directly. It's often used in a contemptuous way for someone who's unwilling to state a personal opinion, or come down
one way or another on an issue. This might play well in the
social and political arenas, but it's painful and unproductive in
the workplace.

Some qualification is unavoidable, especially when the information you're imparting is based upon the actions of people
you can't control, or you're simply uncertain. But again, you
can avoid the worst of the problem by delivering your communications without frills. Don't ramble. Avoid uncertainty
or hesitation. Use the active tense rather than the passive.
Say things like, "I need this file . . ." rather than "This file is
needed . . . ," because it sounds more direct and imperative.
Give people a deadline by which you need results, not "if you
get the chance," or "when you can."

Similarly, if someone asks you a question, give them the
specific information they've requested, rather than a dump of
your entire brain. You can be helpful and add additional information if you think it's relevant, but don't waste your time or
theirs with extraneous information.

Make your requests and requirements plain. Workplace communication should be as unambiguous as humanly possible. Directness is important when asking for information or giving instructions. Take charge, choose authoritative words, and make your requirements absolutely clear.

In an effort to say the minimum possible, however, be careful about being unclear. If you tell someone, "I need information on the Smith account," you're direct, all right; but you're too vague, because you haven't asked for enough information. Which Smith account do you mean? If two or three Smiths exist with different first names, you're already tripping over the speed bump of uncertainty. Furthermore, what material do you need—everything in the whole file, or just this year's financials? And when do you need it—within the next hour, by the close of business, or sometime in the next week?

So don't hesitate to explain as much as required for others to fully understand you, especially in terms of deadlines and deliverables required. Just don't unload so much information on your listeners that they can't understand what you're saying. This is a judgment call, and planning and pre-editing your message is helpful here. Examine your message closely before sending. If all they really need to know is in the final line of the message, then cut everything else and just send the final line.

It's also important to use the right words to get the point across. If what you're trying to say doesn't seem quite on the mark, then spend some time refining it, because it's likely to pay off in dividends of greater comprehension. As Mark Twain once pointed out, "The difference between the right word and the almost-right word is the difference between lightning and lightning-bug."

In general, make your language easy to understand. Don't address someone as though they're a third-grader, but on the other hand, don't use ten-dollar words just because you can. Also avoid using unnecessary jargon. Before you refer to something by an acronym or an abbreviation, make sure it's a shared term. For example: It won't help to ask a new intern to get you the RFP for the DFW DCH account ASAP if they don't know that an RFP is a Request for Proposal, and DFW DCH is shorthand for the Dallas/Fort Worth branch of the Dalquist, Culpepper, and Harrison law firm.

Acknowledgment in all directions. In the military, someone who receives a verbal order is often required to repeat it back immediately to acknowledge they received it. This is especially true in the Navy. It's Standard Operating Procedure (SOP) for a simple reason: If a message is poorly relayed and the wrong action taken, the results can be disastrous.

Your miscommunications may not have devastating results, but they can certainly damage productivity. Therefore, acknowledgment of those communications is absolutely essential. When you receive a message from someone, whether they're above or below you in the chain of command, acknowledge its receipt as quickly as possible, even if you can't supply the answer immediately.

Similarly, request acknowledgment and an estimated time of completion from anyone with whom you correspond; if they don't respond, ping them again in a few days. No need for rudeness, just assertiveness and persistence. Send them an e-mail nudge or pick up the phone and say, "Hey, I sent you a message about such-and-such. Did you get it?" It's possible they didn't. Maybe it passed under their radar due to disorganization, or the technology you sent it by simply failed you in this instance. That happens occasionally, as all of us can attest.

You can't let anyone use the claim they didn't get a message as an excuse for not getting something done. Get an acknowledgment—not so you can cover yourself later, but so you can make sure they understand what you need and require, and so you know they comprehend the urgency of your request.

In a related vein, make it clear that people can ask questions if they don't understand what you're trying to say. Encourage them to request clarification, and be patient when they do; if you don't, their lack of understanding will result in unproductive errors and rework. The same goes for you: If you don't understand exactly what your requester wants, keep asking questions until you do—even in the face of their irritation. It's more productive to go back and forth a few times than to find out later you did something incorrectly due to a miscommunication.

While the potential for confusion always exists in human interaction, solid, clear communication at all levels will make sure such confusion is minimized. If you follow these simple rules, not only will people not have to waste time (and therefore productivity) trying to figure out what you're trying to say, but also they are less likely to mistake what you're trying to say. Mistakes waste time, and time really is money—so it's crucial to avoid as many miscommunications as possible.

🕐 If someone doesn't acknowledge a communication, repeat it. If they still don't respond, contact them through another medium. If they keep ignoring you, go over their head or around them.

HANDLING MICROMANAGERS

In the modern workplace, perhaps the worst people-related plague—and certainly one of the most common hindrances to closing a workflow loop and simply getting anything done— is micromanaging. According to recent statistics, a whopping 75–80 percent of American workers have suffered under micromanagers at some point. One-third of us have changed jobs because of them.[22]

Micromanagers, for those of you fortunate enough to have never encountered one, are bosses who don't trust you to get your job done. They keep a constant eye on you, interfering with how you work, sending incessant instructions on how to do every little thing, and hovering at your elbow all day long. They're obsessed with detail and refuse to let you take the initiative in anything, forcing you to check in with them before making any decision or beginning any new task. Ultimately, their distrust in your ability to do your job becomes a self-fulfilling prophecy, because they don't *let* you do your job.

So how do you deal with them? How do you handle them on a daily basis, and keep them from absolutely destroying your productivity?

This is one of those situations where you have to tread carefully, tailoring any advice to your individual personality and situation. Various experts have taken differing approaches to the subject, suggesting numerous (and often contradictory) ways of dealing with micromanagers. The only thing they agree on is you're unlikely to change a micromanager's ways, because as a category, they derive pleasure from trying to control your every move.

Personally, I'm not sure this is *always* the case. If you feel your boss is micromanaging you, take a hard look at yourself first. Are you new to the job? How does your performance compare to others in your group? Do your coworkers feel the same way about the boss? As hard as it is to admit, perhaps you're giving your manager legitimate reasons to micromanage you. Buckle down, focus on your productivity, and see if things improve.

On the other hand, I agree there's a certain level of petty tyranny involved in most micromanaging. When this is the case, you basically have three choices: You can adapt, find another job, or confront them directly.

Adapting may involve anything from appeasement to manipulating your micromanager to your satisfaction. Admittedly, appeasement isn't ideal; I wouldn't consider it unless your situation is desperate and you need to "play the game." You also have the option of micromanaging the micromanager. In other words, try to overwhelm them with the minutiae they typically require until they're sick of it. Find out precisely what they want, and get it to them ahead of time. Be relentless. Keep in constant contact. Follow the rules precisely and preempt deadlines.

Some authorities recommend trying to prove to the micromanager that you're capable of doing your job. The idea is to take on a new role or project and roll it out perfectly, so they'll see the error of their ways and back off. This rarely works. Micromanagers are all about control and have an ingrained lack of trust. Even a minor mistake can be fatal: They'll focus on it as proof they were right to micromanage you in the first place, no matter how well you've done otherwise.

Whatever you do, document your interactions with micromanagers. Have them write down their requirements for you. Record orders in a journal (written or electronic), and be very specific as to dates and times. Carefully track everything you do to fulfill orders. When something goes wrong, you can pull out your notes and say, "Well, here's what you told me to do on such-and-such a date." While having to track everything this way may seem abysmally unproductive, in the end it may help you protect yourself—especially if they try to pin the blame for something on you.

If you can't live with being micromanaged, and you can't find a way to successfully manage your manager, you always have the option of leaving that environment. Either transfer elsewhere in the organization or find a new opportunity. Some experts recommend against this, claiming it's self-defeating. They argue that since micromanagers are everywhere, you might end up working for another one after you change jobs. Not to mention that it can be difficult to find another job in times of high unemployment and economic uncertainty.

This is a bit like saying that even if your chickenpox is cured, you might just catch measles. True . . . but conversely, you might end up healthier and more productive than ever before. If you must leave to maintain your sanity, then leave. If you just can't seem to escape the micromanagement trap even after changing jobs, look within. Perhaps consider starting your own business, so you never have to worry about others managing you again.

The best option is to schedule a meeting with your manager, and politely but firmly point out that you can't work productively in an environment where you're treated as though you're untrustworthy. Emphasize your desire for a more empowered and professional work environment. Outline the checkpoints and how you'd like to be evaluated. You may find a positive response to your request. But if instead your manager starts citing personal strict standards, and how no one can be allowed the slightest bit of slack, you're unlikely to ever get through.

REDUCING INEFFICIENCIES AND BREAKING BOTTLENECKS

The Productivity Workflow Formula allows for constant re-evaluation and change, so you can reduce all inefficiencies inherent to your job. As time passes, the circle will become smaller as you tighten your methods.

Never assume the way you do things is the best possible way to do them; in fact, it probably isn't. There's almost always a better way. So take the new information you've acquired, use it to create more efficient processes, and put those processes to work. Even as you implement the new processes, you'll find some are more effective than others. So actively evaluate what works and what doesn't, and weed out the poor producers.

In many cases, a broken process isn't flawed. A few tweaks may transform it into something useful and productive. So when something fails you, start by asking questions to figure out why.

- What changes can you make to improve the methods and procedures you're using?
- What can you do to work more effectively?

- What's holding you back?
- What new systems are benefiting your life?
- What's frustrating you?
- What's keeping you from doing what you know you should be doing?
- What obstacles do you perceive?

Constant analysis will help you to find inefficiencies in your schedule so you can reduce them and thereby increase productivity.

In addition to finding and clearing internal inefficiencies, you'll also want to look for bottlenecks—external factors slowing your workflow. If you regularly commute or drive busy freeways, you know how much a bottleneck can slow progress. When four lanes of traffic suddenly funnel into one, slowing is inevitable, even if everyone is driving effectively and efficiently. Your workflow may have similar bottlenecks, so identify them and make plans to break them.

Real-World Examples

If something's cutting into your productivity, you must work to change it—no two ways about it.

Often the required change is relatively small and simple to implement. For example, I once bought a handheld, which worked fine for a while. Over time, I discovered it would connect to my e-mail server only if it had a really full battery charge. This wasn't a problem if I remembered to plug it in every night; but one night I didn't, and the next day I was out on appointments and couldn't get my messages. The battery was internal and couldn't be replaced easily. My one-year warranty was over, but I wasn't yet in the two-year window required for an upgrade. In frustration, I bought the newer model at full price, and the difference was amazing. I asked myself, "Why didn't I do this sooner?" I couldn't believe I put up with this situation for so long for a few measly extra bucks.

I wondered what other irritations I was tolerating and

found several things I could easily change: a slow printer; an uncomfortable chair; a keyboard with a stuck "l" key I had to hit hard several times, and so on. It's amazing how many personal inefficiencies we tolerate on a daily basis!

Sometimes workflow inefficiencies can have organization-wide repercussions as well. In the 1970s, for example, IBM was having a huge problem selling computer mainframes. Everyone wanted to buy one, so desire wasn't a problem. They could manufacture them fast enough, so speed to delivery wasn't the issue either. Of all things, the processing of credit approvals was taking an average of six weeks!

Therefore, a bright sales engineer decided to run a test: He hand-carried a credit application through the entire approval process. He made people stop what they were doing and deal with the application immediately. As a result, he pushed the application through in forty-five minutes, instead of the normal six weeks. All he did was eliminate the bottlenecks in the system.

Many, if not most, systems have inherent bottlenecks. Unfortunately, we usually can't see them without taking the time to step back and look at the bigger picture. It's one of those "can't see the forest for the trees" situations.

So how do you identify the inefficient processes in your workplace? It's actually rather simple. Think about this question: What do you dread because of the length of time it takes? If it's annoying you, there's a good chance that there's something inefficient in the process. Take a good look at it, with the idea of finding where valuable time is being wasted by you or others.

Remember, no matter how you're doing it, there's always a better way. As long as you keep that attitude in mind, you'll keep analyzing, seeking to come up with that better way. Instead of looking at new technology and new methodologies and saying "That's nice," look at them and ask yourself, "How can this help me be more productive?"

When you find better ways to do things, try them out. Experiment with your new processes and systems to see if they really work. Sometimes the most ridiculous-sounding things work wonderfully well, and the most logical ones are failures. So don't let your mind throw something away just because it doesn't sound as though it will work—test it first. Likewise, don't become wedded to any particular idea. Just because it sounds good doesn't mean it's workable. It may be a lemon.

The good ideas are the ones that work; ultimately, that's the only criterion that matters. Even then, don't assume you can't improve a good idea. The time to start improving any process is as soon as you have it in place and working.

The Human Factor

Many workflow bottlenecks are human rather than procedural; all too often, the actions of our coworkers (or lack thereof) cause the process to spring a leak. We frequently need data, additional materials, or approval from another person before we can proceed with our piece of a project. Maybe you can't begin your task until someone else hands something off to you; however, that person isn't as worried about meeting the deadline as you are, so yours gets pushed back even further. Or maybe you encounter constant discrepancies in someone's work that require rework or clarification. In either case, your ability to move forward is dependent upon the other's person's performance.

While some human bottlenecks are beyond your control, you may be able influence others. Ask the person causing you problems, "What can I do to help you get this done?" While you may ask your question in all honesty and with a helpful attitude, you're also letting the person know that they *are* a problem. Now, most human bottlenecks don't like being told they're bottlenecks. Typically, they'll respond in one of two ways: anger or complaints. Anger usually means they're the direct source of the bottleneck (hence the bad attitude). Complaints usually mean something else is causing a bottleneck for them. In the latter case, it may turn out that a piece of

---

🕐 Even if you can't tweak a particular process into
usefulness, it may be possible to merge it with another idea
that didn't quite work and come up with something that does.

---

equipment, a procedural change, or a suggestion is all it takes
to eliminate the problem.

On the other hand, some things just take time to complete.
Let those bottlenecks go and move on to others you can fix.
But before leaving such a bottleneck, get an estimated completion date. By doing so, you commit the other person to action
and know when to follow up. Don't forget about it, but don't
worry about it either.

Teamwork Tips

When you're part of a team, each teammate affects your productivity and how quickly things get done. When others are
late in getting answers to you, you're late in producing the final product. When you rely on coworkers to review a document before proceeding, a month can go by before you have
everyone's input. It's in your best interest to help your team
members get things done more quickly, so you can produce
better results in less time with fewer frustrations.

One way to increase everyone's response time is to arrange a meeting with your team members at the beginning
of a project, so you can plan it through to the end. As much as
we all hate meetings, they're worth the time if you can keep
dependencies from clogging the workflow later. Lay out the
milestones, clearly communicate each team member's responsibilities, and set firm deadlines. Outline what you need from
each person and have them do the same for you. Do your best
to be flexible in all directions, and establish contingency plans
that will allow you to work around emergencies, illness, and
other unexpected occurrences.

If your team consists of individuals in diverse locations, teams, or organizations, you'll have to work harder to limit potential bottlenecks. In each case, negotiate very clear agreements on when you need to receive information, materials, or approvals. Politely explain your deadlines and the reasoning behind them, and ask when the team member might be able to provide what you need. Reinforce (in a genial, non-pushy way) the importance of what you're asking, and why their active participation in the project is crucial. This may shore up their motivation, since we all like to feel needed and appreciated.

Contingency planning is even more important with team members you don't work with directly; so if possible, establish alternate means of acquiring what you need. That way, if your primary source is away from the office, or occupied by a higher-priority project, you can turn to the backup for help.

Make contingency plans for your own unavailability as well. Coordinate with a coworker to handle your part of a project if you're unavailable, and make sure your project resources are easily accessible and understandable.

Helping You Helps Me

I hate to use a tired old business cliché, but you really do need to think outside the box to make sure the workflow process continues uninterrupted. You should be willing to grease the skids a little whenever things slow to a crawl. Let me give you an example of such streamlining from my own business.

My assistant, Becca, frequently received calls from our clients asking her to send wording they could use to introduce me to audiences at speaking engagements. Ninety-nine percent of the time, she had already sent the information. Even though her job is customer service, it can be frustrating and time-consuming to provide the same information repeatedly.

I uncovered the problem one day when she was joking about how a particular client chronically lost information she'd already sent—possibly the very reason the client had hired me in the first place.

So we brainstormed a solution and decided to post *everything* a client might need on our website, so customers could. help themselves to the information they needed without involving her. Every time a customer requested information, we added it to our site. Once we updated the website, we proactively sent links to our clients telling them where they could find this information. Becca now fulfills far fewer manual client requests.

This kind of "I'm on your side" approach saves everyone time and frustration. You're basically saying, "Help us help you." Actively pursue these opportunities to eliminate nagging time bandits, frustrations, and productivity-sappers from your systems every day. Doing so boosts your productivity, builds solidarity with your colleagues and clients, and shows you're willing to listen to and implement their ideas.

So at your next staff meeting, get some time on the agenda to pose three questions:

1. *What are the three most mind-numbing, time-wasting hoops you must jump through on a weekly basis?* And then listen to the responses. Don't get defensive or combative. Instead, scribble down everything people say and soak it in.

2. *What time-draining procedures or activities do you find yourself doing more than three times a week?* The purpose of this question is to identify the "debris" littering your coworkers' high-speed highway and slowing them down repeatedly. You'll also discover redundancy if multiple people do the same thing.

3. *How can we help you get things done more quickly?* Brainstorm ways to automate your systems and reduce wasted time, so you can all get your work done faster, leave the office earlier, and get home to your lives.

🕐 To clear the path to greater group productivity, meet only when absolutely necessary—and then only briefly.

Just think about the innovative thinking that could take place! Make it your goal to help others blast through time-wasting obstacles. By helping them, you help yourself.

Driving Change

While it's great if you can get your coworkers and team members on board with any new systems and procedures you implement, don't worry too much about those who don't join you. Many people are so attached to their old ways of doing things they'd rather die doing them that way. I'm sure you've seen it: the old "We've always done it this way" attitude. I'd say if you've always done it that way, it's probably time to change it.

The best way to bring about change in your organization is to let management see you're more productive than anyone else—they'll want everyone to adopt your systems. You won't have to try to convince them; they'll come to you and ask.

When you reduce inefficiencies, you become a true asset to the organization for which you work. Your improvements and advances will quickly become the standard by which the organization rates everyone else's work. That makes you the expert in the organization.

THE QUEST FOR CONSTANT IMPROVEMENT

To consistently close the loop in your workflow process, make constant, unremitting efforts at improvement. Strive to exceed your own standards of performance for yourself, whether those standards are obvious to anyone else or not. It's all too easy to slack off a little here and there when no one's really paying attention.

When he was ten years old, my son Johnny took guitar lessons from a teacher named Michael. One week Johnny taught himself to play the song "Sweet Home Alabama" and practiced it for hours. When Johnny showed off his new song to his teacher, Michael said, "Hey, that's great! Here's how you can play it even a little better," and showed him how to do a riff. To Michael's surprise, Johnny was resistant to learning it.

When I pressed Johnny about what was wrong after Michael left, he told me, "Well, none of my friends play the guitar, so they won't know if I'm doing a bad job. They think it's cool no matter what I play, so I don't need to work so hard to change it."

I shook my head, a bit baffled, and gave him the "mom" talk about how personal improvement is also done for the sake of it, not just for other people; you take pride in knowing you did your best at something; we should always strive to get better; besides, when you're an adult, at some point you'll run up against people who *will* know if you're doing a bad job, blah, blah, blah. I'm not sure how much it sank in, but the thought occurred to me that many parents *didn't* give their children this lecture, and now those children are grown up and in the workplace.

Always try to do better, even if no one else knows, even if what you're doing is "good enough," and even if the only beneficiaries of trying harder are you and your family. You'll save your health and sanity by trimming your workflow process to the bare minimum, and you'll have pride in your work. The more you keep chipping away at it, the more efficient you can become.

🕐 Whenever you can spare a little extra time, polish one of your critical productivity skills. Focus on one at a time, and never accept just good enough as good enough.

Rising from the Ashes

Now, a few (hundred) words about failure. Let's face it: Implementing the PWF won't come without its hitches. You're going to slam into walls occasionally as you attempt to initiate change and reduce inefficiencies. Not everything is going to work out for you, and sometimes you may want to give up.

In the modern business world, failure is often touted as something glorious, a virtue that almost inevitably leads to success. Oft-cited examples include Edison's 1,000+ unsuccessful attempts to invent the lightbulb before hitting on the right solution, and Bill Gates's unsuccessful first computer business. The experts tell us again and again to fail forward, to fail as fast as possible, and to dare to fail, because it makes us smarter and better in the long run.

So it was rather disconcerting to run across a recent working paper called "Performance Persistence in Entrepreneurship" that takes the opposite tack.[23] The authors scrutinized a large sample of venture capital–backed IPOs and discovered that brand-new entrepreneurs succeeded about as often as those who had tried before and failed (18 percent vs. 20 percent, respectively). The most successful entrepreneurs were those who had already succeeded: serial entrepreneurs, as they called them. But even serial entrepreneurs succeeded only about 30 percent of the time.

At the risk of oversimplification, the authors basically pointed out that statistically, failure doesn't necessarily result in eventual success—a common-sense "no duh" conclusion, frankly. Furthermore, the authors admitted they looked at a relatively narrow business segment. They failed to control for a number of factors that might skew the results. So normally, I'd take something like this with a grain of salt.

However, the paper actually tested the assumption that failure is positive in the long run. Commentators who have written about the paper are quick to point out that there's no real scholarly work that proves that failure is good for the soul;

we just assume that it is. On the other hand, there's now research that suggests that failure doesn't necessarily contribute to later success.

While I do believe you should focus on things you're good at, I also believe failure can be helpful in defining the things you're bad at and should *never* do again because they are a waste of time. In general, then, the concept of failure helping you succeed in the long run is a truism and therefore doesn't require scholarly proof. For example, my high-school daughter dislikes science immensely; she doesn't do well at it without a lot of effort. She's a 4.0 student and wants to go to business school, so it makes sense for her to take as little science as she needs to get into the university she wants to attend. Why would she purposefully take a class that's difficult, that she hates, and that she has no interest in in the future? To me, that's counter-productive.

I'm convinced failure *can* help you succeed, but it won't do so automatically. Failure does not anoint you with the oil of future success. Some of my colleagues have gone a little too far in suggesting it does . . . or in outright saying so.

There's nothing special about failure itself; it's what you *do* with failure that matters. So be willing to risk failure while fine-tuning your workflow process. Don't be afraid of it. Failure is just another opportunity to learn; this allows you to rise phoenix-like from the ashes, to take another grab at the brass ring. Maybe you'll get it this time; maybe you won't. But if not, don't take the failure itself too personally, because it kills your confidence and destroys your chances to learn from your mistakes. Make every effort to take something instructive away from your failure, or you've just wasted your time.

🕑 Don't fear failure, but don't assume it's inevitable. Fortune favors the bold, so once you've made your basic preparations, dive right in, and deal with the details as they arise.

The truth is, as long as you can survive a failure, there's almost always some tidbit you can pull from the wreckage and take to heart. There may be a few intact bricks left standing—successful aspects or ideas within the broader failure—that can serve as a foundation for building a new edifice.

I'm not going to tell you there's no such thing as a failure; of course there is. But don't ignore failure, refusing to learn anything, and hope to luck into success. Failure to learn from failure will inevitably lead to more failure, in a vicious downward spiral. Refuse to allow it to happen to you!

CONTINUED PROGRESS REQUIRES CONSTANT REEVALUATION

Once your new workflow process is up and running, keep a high-level eye on its operation and tweak your systems toward perfection at every opportunity. Effectively closing the loop requires tight organization and a willingness to jump in immediately and fix what isn't working optimally. Constant reevaluation is critical for continued progress, so scrutinize all your tasks regularly, looking for easier, faster ways to do them.

Respond to external feedback quickly, pinpoint any recurring problems, and work toward eliminating them. Smooth over rough patches. Replace missing pieces or "worn" parts that no longer work properly. Immediately purge and replace anything wasting your time. If you need to institute a major change, or something just isn't working out, you may want to take a little time off to retool all or part of your system. If you find yourself in over your head, then by all means, seek help! In any case, learn from your mistakes along the way . . . and then let them go.

No matter how difficult it may seem, don't give up. Any effort to maintain peak performance will inevitably require trial and error. As you try new strategies, some will work well, and others will fall short. Things may go awry and grind to a halt occasionally, because you can't account for everything;

🕐 Keep an eye on your productivity metrics. The numbers will tell you what works and what you need to fix.

but again, don't let that stop you from trying. Learning to reduce your commitments to a manageable level, and building your daily time savings to a full ninety minutes will take time, and even the most well-tuned machine needs maintenance occasionally. The Productivity Workflow Formula will require ongoing refinement, and occasionally, some larger-scale reworking.

Keep your motivation high by remembering your goal. If you persevere, you *will* succeed, and you *will* find time for yourself and skyrocket your results. You'll soon start to notice the difference these changes are making in your life. You'll have more time and more energy, because you won't be wasting your day on unneeded tasks. Those ninety minutes or more per day that you'll be able to set aside for yourself will make a huge difference in all aspects of your life.

SUMMARY: PWF STEP 5 CHECKUP

Once you've learned how to triage your commitment load, schedule your tasks appropriately, focus your attention, and process new information, it's time to consolidate everything into a single, efficient, time-saving system.

Closing the loop means tinkering with your workflow until all the components work smoothly together, weeding out the unnecessary at every turn and replacing anything that doesn't work as well as it should. Begin by creating a plan of action to organize your life and workspace for maximum efficiency, clearing the clutter, and doing all you can to minimize the effort and time you spend on basic processes.

You can't avoid all the human factors that may inhibit your

workflow, but do your best to limit confusion by making sure you communicate clearly and with a minimum of "noise." Get straight to the point, avoid hedging, make your needs plain, and require acknowledgment in all directions.

If you find yourself faced with micromanagers, do what you can to work around or accommodate them, so they don't completely ruin your productivity. If necessary, confront them politely but directly with your inability to work under the conditions they impose; they may back off.

You'll inevitably face workflow inefficiencies and bottle-necks, some of which derive from inefficient processes you can either upgrade or replace. Again, however, people often cause such blockages. Whatever the case, step in immediately, and do your best to put them right. If you can't clear a bottleneck, don't obsess over it; maneuver around it and move on to what you *can* fix.

In the modern workplace, teamwork is especially important; so like it or not, you may find yourself depending on others to keep your workflow steady. Strive to make it easy for everyone involved. Start by clarifying the group workflow process, providing milestones and deadlines, and assigning tasks to particular individuals. Set up contingency plans for handling crises and emergencies, especially when dealing with people in other organizations.

All in all, you must continually tighten your workflow loop, making consistent efforts to maximize your efficiency. Constantly evaluate what works and what doesn't, learn from your mistakes, fill in the gaps as they occur, and keep reaching toward the brass ring of doing less and achieving greater results.

6

Manage Your Capacity

This sixth and final step appears at the center of the PWF for a simple but powerful reason: It's the hub holding everything together. If you can't manage your capacity, your workflow will eventually stall or fall apart. Step Six is the most critical aspect of the entire process, because it underlies, supports, and influences all the other steps. Without it, nothing else is possible.

Many things can affect your ability to manage your capacity, but the most important factor is *you*: your health, your determination, and your energy level. So in this chapter, I'll focus on the physical and mental factors directly affecting your capacity to remain productive throughout the day.

This final stage in the PWF makes everything else worth the effort. Throughout this book, you've learned to scale back and reduce, reduce, reduce. You've found ways to reduce your to-do list, your calendar commitments, distractions, information overload, and inefficiencies. Each reduction will increase your results and save you time. Learning to do less but to accomplish more will bring many benefits to you, your family, and your organization. And isn't that what all that energy and activity is about?

PERSONAL ENERGY

Energy is capacity: the potential to do work, to enjoy life, and to achieve your goals. Energy affects everything—it's the very axis on which your productivity spins.

Fortunately, you have the potential to dramatically affect your personal energy levels, and hence your productivity, simply by paying close attention to your health. When you feel well, you can accomplish more. But many people eat too much, drink too much, work too much, don't exercise enough, and don't sleep enough. It's not surprising they're less than fully productive when tired or ill: It's hard to remain productive if you feel like putting your head down on your desk and taking a nap.

So never lose sight of this fact: If you don't practice good self-care, you won't be able to muster the energy required to practice the PWF on a daily basis. Therefore, take care of yourself in every way you can. Learn to reduce your energy expenditure, take breaks as you need them, get enough rest, eat properly, exercise regularly, and manage your mental health.

Imagine how much you could accomplish if at the end of your day, you still had extra energy. Would boosting your productivity boost your profits? How would the time you spend with your friends and family change? Instead of collapsing on the couch the instant you got home, what would it be like if you had the ability to focus on your loved ones? What if there was a way to accelerate your efficiency at work so you could devote more time to making memories with the people you love?

Reduce Your Energy Expenditure

Are you allowing exhaustion to cripple you? Are you burning more energy than you can spare? In the American workplace, we've finally managed to overcome the idea of burning the candle at both ends . . . but only by replacing it with the idea of burning the candle at both ends *and* in the middle. While lauded by managers as a way of squeezing a few more minutes of work out of their employees, all this is really doing is making their employees tired. Too many people are trying to achieve success by working longer, when really they're just spending more hours doing the same amount of work. Their productivity isn't going up—work quality is going down as energy levels plummet.

I've seen the devastating effects of plunging energy levels. I've watched and listened to clients and friends pour out their hearts in private about the anxiety, the guilt, the fatigue, the shame, and yes, even the serious depression they've privately felt for spinning aimlessly on the "hamster wheel of life."

Perhaps you're chasing after achievement rainbows in the hopes of finding pots of gold, destroying yourself in the process. If so, your lack of energy, extreme exhaustion, and inefficient, unproductive practices may be robbing your soul of the greatest joys life has to offer.

The Law of Diminishing Returns

You lose productivity rather than increase it when you overextend yourself. You're not a machine; you can't work more hours and produce more just because you decide not to turn off your power switch. In fact, productivity drops off drastically after eight hours on the job. When you think about it, it's clear that in many cases doing less work, rather than more, is the better, more fruitful choice.

Let's say you're working on a rush project and decide to put in eleven-hour days for the next three weeks to finish it. How much do you *really* think you're going to get done in those

---

⊕ Instead of being depressed because you can't perform at superhuman levels all the time, readjust your expectations to fit your energy levels, and stop running your "battery" dry.

---

extra three hours per day? Let's say your productivity drops by 25 percent after eight hours of non-stop work. Then, because you're not going to get enough rest, it will fall another 25 percent for every hour after the first eight. Basically, your productivity is cut in half after the first eight hours of work. For three extra hours a day for five days, you'll put in an extra fifteen hours, but it's only the equivalent of seven and a half hours. So in those fifty-five hours, you'll have actually netted forty-seven and a half hours of work (assuming everything goes smoothly). You've spent fifteen extra hours to get seven and a half hours—not a great return on investment.

Oh, and by the way, the extra time you spend at work increases your chance of a heart attack by 67 percent.[24] Is it really worthwhile to work those extra hours when the biggest return you're likely to get for them is a heart attack?

Bouncing Back

Imagine preparing to run a marathon. You know the marathon will require a lot of training and will expend a lot of your energy. After months of training and preparation, months of pushing yourself right to the wall, the marathon day arrives. Do you hit the gym before you head to the course? Of course not! You need to be rested. Your body has limits, and if you're already pushing those limits by running a marathon, you would never try to add more stress.

Handle your life and your schedule in the same manner. Know your limits and stick to them. This workflow process is all about helping you to achieve success while living within those limits. You'll attain greater results while working less, have extra time to enjoy life, and end each day feeling better.

You *can* achieve without overdoing it, and you can start by learning to do the most you can with the energy you already have. Each of us has a finite amount of energy to spend during the day. You could say it's your battery. Not all batteries are equal; so some people can expend more energy in a workday than others. Some people are more efficient at expending physical energy, and some are more adept at mentally challenging tasks. Regardless, at the end of the day, the battery is drained until it's recharged. You can't use more energy than you have.

Your goal is to equalize your energy expenditure with the level of available energy in your batteries. If you're drained, your performance will show it. Your options are to either reduce your energy expenditure, or increase your battery power.

Don't try to turn into superman or superwoman; be yourself. Learn to recognize your body's signs of tiredness and listen to them. Set realistic goals of what you can accomplish each day, and then reduce your daily tasks until they can fit within your limits. If you have too much to do, use the triage method described in Chapter 1 to prioritize and cut things out of your to-do lists. Don't push yourself into working beyond your limits. No matter what other people think of your schedule, the reality is that you can push yourself only so far. Too much time at work eats into the energy reserves your body uses to keep you healthy.

🕐 If you spend a lot of time fixing your own mistakes, you may be working more hours than you can bodily handle. Do you need to cut back on your work schedule, or do you need to repair your energy habits—or both?

The Value of Breaks, Large and Small

No matter how spectacular you are, you can only grind along at maximum focus for so long before you get tired and mistakes start creeping into your work . . . and then your productivity drops like a rock. While there can be such a thing as too many breaks, you do need to pull back occasionally to recharge your creativity and energy. You do your best work when you're well-rested. Bodies simply need time for relaxation and recuperation; there's no practical way around it. So set aside periods of time for restoring your body and taking care of yourself.

First of all, step away from your work occasionally during the day; this is why most state labor laws mandate brief breaks in the morning and afternoon. At the very least, your breaks will clear your mental buffers and help maintain your energy.

Meal breaks are also important. Eat something small every few hours. If you go longer than six hours without eating, your blood sugar levels will drop, and you may become fuzzy-headed. So don't skip lunch or just scarf down a sandwich at your desk. Try to get away for a few minutes. A change in scenery and pace will help you stay sharp.

Don't skip your macro-breaks, either. Take your weekends, holidays, and vacations as often as possible, so you can rest. When work rolls around again, you'll have a fresh charge. Time away from work is an important part of personal productivity, because it's during this time our batteries get fully recharged, rather than half-charged. Just expecting to recuperate while you're thinking about work in front of the television set won't work. To completely recharge your batteries, get your mind off work and do something more enjoyable.

This is easier said than done for some people, who get worried about taking a vacation. They worry they won't be missed; or they dread the volume of work facing them upon their return; or they think a vacation reflects negatively on their commitment to the organization. But once you return and realize the world didn't fall apart and you didn't get fired, you might wonder what took you so long. Open your calendar and plan to get away soon! The true source of productivity isn't nonstop output; it's a refreshed and energized mind, a vacation's specialty. Wasn't recess your favorite part of elementary school?

Our family loves vacations, and we take them often. In 2006, my husband and I took a vacation to Hawaii, sans children, in Kailua-Kona on the Big Island. It was a busy time for our business, and I was wondering what would fall through the cracks. I promised my husband I would check in at the office

🕐 When you have no choice but to overwork yourself,
try to do so in short bursts separated by longer periods
of normal work—or rest. Otherwise, you'll soon hit the
wall, and your productivity will diminish sharply.

only once a day, early in the morning, as I preach to my audiences. It turned out it wasn't hard to follow my own advice.

Hawaii was four hours earlier than my internal clock, so I was bright-eyed and bushy-tailed and ready to go . . . at 3:00 A.M. It took several days for my body to adjust and remain alert past 8:30 P.M. So while my hubby was still sleeping soundly, I would log on, talk with my office manager, check my e-mail and voicemail, and get ready for relaxation or adventure by the time he woke up.

It's amazing how unimportant things seemed in Hawaii— things I might have jumped on right away while in the office. I just told people I was in Hawaii and would handle it when I got back. Everyone understood and told me to enjoy myself.

We were alone for eight wonderful days, and it really stretched my mind, recharged my energy, and rested my soul. It was definitely worth the pile of work I was buried beneath upon my return. I didn't lose any business, the kids didn't break any bones, and nothing of any consequence happened. I worried for nothing. So take a deep breath, fight your fear, and go for a vacation! You'll maintain your energy, your health, and your sanity.

The Payoff

Reducing your energy expenditure doesn't always mean accomplishing less. In many cases, you can find ways to do the same tasks more efficiently. For example, if you combine a client meeting with lunch, you're taking care of two necessary tasks at once. If you need files from the storage room, take a short walk on your way back. Answer all your e-mails a few times a day, rather than checking them every few minutes. There are numerous ways to spend less energy on tasks while accomplishing the same amount of work.

I've designed each step of the PWF process to help you reduce your overall energy expenditure. Part of managing your capacity is to remember your limits while finding ways to streamline what you already do each day. You don't have to sacrifice the important things. Just focus on the few things you really need to do; find the fat in your schedule and trim it out.

GET SOME SLEEP

Are you getting enough sleep? If not, you're basically slamming a wrecking ball through your energy levels.

First, your circadian rhythms are extremely sensitive to the amount of sleep you get each day. As you may know, the word "circadian" is Latin for "about a day." Variously referred to as the "body clock," "master clock," or "biological clock," your circadian rhythms are regulated by the hypothalamus, an area of your brain that controls energy, activity, and how you physically feel. Each day you have to "reset" your body clock, and thus the need for sleep.

Among other things, sleep (or a lack thereof) can have a tremendous effect on mood. A recent analysis of 500 million Twitter messages, published in *Science* magazine, reveal that people all over the world are more likely to express positive emotion in the morning and evenings, with notable dips in between.[25] The researchers believe this daily emotional cycle is influenced by sleep and the above-mentioned circadian rhythms.

In addition, Ben Franklin's advice about "early to bed, early to rise" has proven to be spot on. The earlier you go to bed, the more you'll supercharge your adrenal glands. Your adrenal glands play a huge role in your energy level by manufacturing adrenaline, cortisol, and DHEA (steroid hormones). Cortisol promotes wakefulness; DHEA helps you relax. Sleep deprivation results in the manufacture of too much cortisol, whereas getting plenty of sleep increases the production of DHEA (designed to keep cortisol levels in check). Staying up late one night and sleeping in the following morning doesn't restore your adrenals as well as going to bed well before midnight does.

Furthermore, the human sleep cycle runs in increments of about ninety minutes. If you get only five and a half hours of sleep, you've lopped off your sleep cycle right in the middle, so it's no wonder you feel lethargic. Sleep cycles usually complete at one and a half hours, three hours, four and a half hours, six hours, and seven and a half hours. This is why you sometimes feel refreshed if you awaken before your alarm goes off; but if you fall back asleep, you may feel super groggy when the alarm finally does go off.

More good reasons to get a good night's sleep: according to a recent Harvard study, you need a full night's sleep to achieve the maximum benefit from Stage 2 Non-Rapid Eye Movement (NREM) sleep, which helps you learn motor skills.[26] The last two hours of sleep are critical for this. Plus, getting just one and a half hours less sleep for just one night may reduce your alertness the next day by up to 32 percent, which can have tragic consequences. For example, National Highway Traffic Safety Administration statistics reveal that drowsy driving results in at least 100,000 car crashes, 40,000 injuries, and 1,550 deaths annually.[27]

Thankfully, most of the negative effects of sleep deprivation are less dramatic, if no less debilitating. Here's an interesting one: Sleep deprivation doubles your risk for obesity, since it increases the production of ghrelin, a natural appetite stimulant, and reduces the production of leptin, an appetite suppressant.[28] Bottom line: Not getting enough sleep can actually make you fat!

And finally, your body's ability to fend off infection and sickness is directly linked to sleep. As we all know, nothing

🕐 If you suffer from insomnia, try drinking a soothing herbal tea an hour before bed, or consume some dairy products. Avoid caffeine and sugar after about 2 P.M.

slows us down worse than getting sick. Our bodies make the most immune-strengthening cellular repairs during the last, longest period of REM sleep; this period begins after seven hours of slumber, so you're robbing your body of the best chance to stop illness if you don't sleep more than seven hours.

During sleep, your brain and muscles restore themselves. It's as necessary as eating, exercising, and going to the bathroom. People who are tired can't effectively deal with life's little everyday stressors, and stress can cause insomnia, creating a vicious cycle of low energy. So don't sabotage your productivity by trying to steal a few minutes from Morpheus (the god of dreams, in Greek mythology).

Here are some tips to make it easier to get the sleep you need.

Control the thermostat. The temperature of your room matters. The ideal sleeping temperature is no less than 68° and no more than 72° Fahrenheit. Anything outside this range could affect your sleep.

Shut out the snoring. Although we joke about it, snoring is often a real source of insomnia. My husband snores, so I wear earplugs (my favorite are Hearos). They drown out his snoring and other background noise but still allow me to hear my alarm clock.

Take a power nap. Some of you have discovered the rejuvenating effects of power naps. As a recent study published in the journal *Nature Neuroscience* concluded, most people can boost their afternoon performance on tasks by taking a daytime nap of sixty minutes or less.[29] If you go over sixty minutes, you'll risk grogginess and so-called sleep inertia when you wake up. But the American Academy of Sleep Medicine reminds us of a very important caveat: The value of a lunchtime or afternoon nap applies only to those who have no symptoms of insomnia. So if you think an afternoon nap will catch you up on lost sleep from your snoring spouse, it's not true. That's just sleepy time fuel dumped on the insomnia fire.

Keep your bedroom sleep-related. A sure-fire energy bandit is turning your bed into a second office, meaning your bed is anything but a space for tranquility and enjoyment. You require a positive mental association between sleep and your bed, so that when you get in bed, your brain should tell your body to shut down and go to sleep. But some of us have turned the bed into a work cubicle with cushions. Your TV is blasting over there. Your munchies are sitting right here. Your laptop is humming down here, with a cord snaking across the comforter. Your paperwork is balancing on a pillow over here. Your cordless phone, BlackBerry, and your cell phone are an arm's length away. Associating your bed with a workspace encourages wakefulness, and soon the brain begins to disassociate your bed with sleep. When you're finally ready to go to sleep, it takes you longer, because your brain is essentially confused.

You have to resolve to turn your bedroom into a sleeping sanctuary, where your mind automatically goes to sleep. Conduct any non-sleep activity—eating, watching television, reading, working on your computer—out of bed, preferably in a completely different room. I realize for us business travelers, it's not always possible; but even moving your gadgets and work materials off the bed and onto the hotel work desk is a step in the right direction.

WATCH YOUR DIET

The old saying "you are what you eat" certainly applies to our energy levels. Among other things, the heavier you are, the less energy you're likely to have. Every day, we read about America's growing obesity problem; health and food researchers have become increasingly concerned by our rate of overeating. And, of course, the type of food we use to fuel our bodies is interrelated with our drops in energy. Clearly, we need to cook up some new dietary strategies.

Start by taking a hard, honest look at what you eat. Not what you *think* you eat, but what you *actually* eat. If you keep a food diary for even a week, you'll be amazed at how much energy-stealing junk you'll discover lurking in your diet.

Just as important as what you eat is *how much* you eat—and that's usually too much. Many people are unable to accurately estimate proper portions, especially busy people on the go or those who travel. In fact, most of us don't even seem to realize we're supposed to keep an eye on serving sizes. A *serving* is not the amount you're expected to eat in one *sitting*. It's the weight and portion that correlates with your recommended daily allowance. Food and nutrition scientists find that in our "super-size" culture, we're woefully misinformed about how to estimate proper portions.

So starting today, integrate these portion control tips. Reduce, reduce, reduce!

Put only two things at a time on your plate. A recent study at Cornell University revealed that people who served themselves just two items at a time ate 21 percent less food.[30] Try this tactic when serving yourself food at home or in a buffet line. Getting up more often will make you realize how much you're actually eating.

Cut 500 calories per day out of your diet. This will amount to about one pound per week (depending on your activity level

🕐 Watch what you drink. Stay hydrated, but limit
your intake of coffee and colas. Caffeine has a
diuretic effect that can dehydrate you even more.

and how efficiently you metabolize calories). Basically, you just
need to slow down your rate of eating. The science on this is
interesting. It turns out it takes approximately twenty minutes
for your brain to receive the "I'm stuffed" signal. So if you're
eating at a restaurant, try going somewhere else for dessert.
Chances are, by the time you get there, you won't want that
Mt. Everest-sized brownie fudge sundae.

Eat a salad before your meal. Researchers at Penn State
found that subjects racked up an average of 12 percent fewer
calories when they ate a salad as their meal's first course.[31] So
serve up a salad, go with the low-fat dressing, and hold the
cheese.

Change your dinnerware to reflect correct portions. Try
using a ten-inch salad plate for your meal instead of a regular
dinner plate. This trick is an eye-opening change. The visual
effect, and also forcing yourself to make more trips to the stove
for more servings, will help cut down on overeating.

Automatically ask for a box. The next time you order at a
restaurant, before the server even leaves your table, ask him to
box half your meal before he brings it out. Or order one meal
for two people, and ask the wait staff to split it for you in the
kitchen.

One more thing: Always eat your morning meal. There's a
reason why we call it "breakfast": You're breaking your over-
night fast. In fact, don't skip any meals, because it mucks up

the steady flow of glucose. The more you can keep your eating times and routines consistent, the better.

If you do these things, you're on the path to a better, more energetic you.

EXERCISE YOUR BODY

It's ironic, but the less active you are, the less energy you have. Fortunately, exercise can boost your energy even in small doses. Did you know a brisk ten-minute walk not only increases energy, but the effects last up to two hours? If you do it consistently, your energy levels and mood will lift like a balloon.

I believe in making exercise painless and fun, so I suggest you engage in what I call "Subversive Exercise." This lets you turn the everyday, mundane acts of life into heart-happy mini-workouts. For example:

- Park at the far end of the parking lot and walk to the door.
- Walk during your lunch break.
- Walk over to see a colleague rather than sending an e-mail.
- Pace around your office while using a speakerphone.
- Forget the elevator; take the stairs.
- Avoid the moving sidewalk at the airport.
- Take the kids out for a family walk after dinner.
- When the kids are playing sports, walk around the perimeter of the field while watching them.
- Watch TV from your treadmill.
- Go to a copy machine or restroom on a different floor.
- Walk around the house while talking on a cordless phone.
- Do squats or leg lunges while reading an article in a magazine or newspaper.

You can use these little tricks to encourage yourself into energy-boosting exercise throughout your day. It doesn't really matter where you work or what you do; being cemented to your chair all day is an energy bandit of the worst kind. So get up, get out, and get your heart pumping and your blood circulating!

Whether you practice Subversive Exercise or stay true to your workout routine, create rewards for yourself. For example, allow yourself to listen to your iPod only when working out. If you want to watch the television, walk on your treadmill in front of it. Get an audio book of a novel you're dying to read, but let yourself listen to it only when exercising. Or tape your favorite show and let yourself watch it only while working out. You get the idea. If you dangle your favorite motivational carrots in front of your face, you'll find yourself sprinting toward the finish line. The biggest prize of all is the blast of energy and productivity you experience.

🕐 Join forces with an "exercise buddy" to help you stay on track, especially if you have trouble maintaining your exercise routine.

MAKE YOURSELF HAPPIER

Rather than let a dour worldview drag you down and ruin your ability to hold it all together, make a conscious decision to adopt a more positive attitude. Do everything you can to make yourself happy and maintain an upbeat outlook. How can you do this? Here are a few ideas you may want to implement.

Make Empowered Choices

Are you an Eeyore? Remember the gloomy ol' donkey from Winnie the Pooh? "Woe is me. Nobody cares if I get swept away in the flood. Not even going to bother trying to swim." Do you know people like this? They throw their hands in the air and act as if there's nothing they can do about their lives.

🕐 Consider joining a professional group, so you can
surround yourself with others who know exactly what
you have to deal with—and who may have some tips
on how to handle those challenges successfully.

These people chalk up their circumstances to fate, a run of bad
luck, or bad karma, when really it's about making poor choices.

You can also make an effort to befriend and surround yourself with positive, upbeat people, both at work and in other aspects of your life. It's a fact that the attitudes of the people you
hang out with have a significant effect on your own attitude.
You won't be able to avoid all the Eeyores out there, but you
can certainly limit your contact with them in favor of bouncy,
optimistic Tiggers!

Make empowering choices to manage your capacity. Life is
too short to be miserable.

Spend More Time with Your Family

Why are you working so hard? If you're like most of us, family
is one of the biggest reasons: You want to provide a good life
for the people you love. This is quite the irony, since working
long hours keeps you away from your family—the very people
for whom you're working so hard to provide. It's too easy to
forget an important fact: the best thing you can spend on the
people you love is *time*.

Besides giving them the attention they need, spending time
with those you love is also a balm for your soul, which allows
you to recharge your energy, so you can continue managing
your capacity.

Letting work intrude on family time is necessary on occa-
sion; but it should be the exception, never the rule. It's important to unplug sometimes for your health and for your loved
ones, who want you to be around. So if you don't want to look

back on your home life with regrets, then it's time to make a bigger hole labeled FAMILY TIME in your schedule, and to build all kinds of barriers around it to keep it sacred. Try to focus exclusively on your family during family time (this will be difficult at first), and work toward ways to give more of yourself to them. Here are some ideas:

- Rearrange your work schedule to be home when they are.
- Take Internet training instead of leaving for days at a time.
- Telecommute a day or two a week.
- Hire household help to take care of basic tasks.
- Have sit-down meals together.
- Occasionally combine business travel with vacations, bringing your family along when you travel for work.
- Limit your kids' extracurricular activities.

Not all of these ideas are possible or even practical for everyone. But they offer a place to start, at least, if you're really serious about spending more time with your family.

Do Something Nice for Someone

Scientists have proven that helping others induces physiological changes in the body. Back in the 1980s, New York City's Institute for the Advancement of Health studied a phenomenon called the "helper's high," an energetic response to helping others that's apparently generated by the release of natural pain relievers called endorphins.[32] The helper's high not only makes you feel better in a purely physical sense, but it also heightens your energy levels and self-esteem. So spend time volunteering: helping at your church, serving at a food bank, painting someone's house, mowing a lawn, or tutoring a student—anything that matches your passion.

Laugh at Adversity

Have you ever had a day where *so* many things went wrong, it started to strike you as downright funny? Your bagel burned.

⊕ Consider mentoring someone new in your field.
Not only will you get a natural high from helping
someone, the teaching process tends to go both ways.
You may just learn a thing or two from your mentee.

Grrrrr. Your six-year-old couldn't find her other shoe, making her ten minutes late for school and you late for work. Grrrrr. You dropped your purse, and the contents spilled out in your car. Grrrrr. The latch popped open on your briefcase, and your paperwork fell in a puddle. Grrrrr. At lunch with a colleague, you shook the ketchup bottle, and a big blob of ketchup landed on your pants. *Hilarious!* This is the stuff comedies are made of! Your entire morning is fodder for a sitcom! You just can't make this stuff up.

I once presented a seminar at an environmental engineering firm. A participant told me a story about an engineer supervising the construction of a wind-monitoring tower for a study involving wind turbines. Something went very wrong, and the 130-foot tower began to crumple the second it was completely upright. While the engineer yelled expletives, one of his coworkers stood right beside him, laughing his head off. The frustrated engineer stared at his coworker in amazement. The coworker said, "Sometimes, all you can do is laugh!" The engineer immediately saw his point and started laughing himself. He knew the next step was simply to start all over again. So he could either wear himself out by continuing to yell expletives or make the best of it by enjoying a much-needed laugh.

Whether you laugh or complain, you won't change the situation. Complaining will make you feel irritable and depressed, drain your energy, and make others stay away from you. Living by the old saying, "Laughter is the best medicine!" is a real energy booster.

🕐 If you ever feel the urge to burst out laughing because
everything's going so badly, share the joke with those
around you, so they know you're not laughing at them.

Surround Yourself with Happiness

What do you surround yourself with to boost your mood?
Some people hang out with happy people, reasoning that the
good vibes will rub off (and they usually do). Some post car-
toons on the office and cubicle walls, or souvenirs from fun
vacations. I have an "I love me" wall with degrees, certificates,
awards, and so on to remind me of accomplishments. I keep
a wall calendar to remind me my job is to keep it filled with
speaking engagements. I have photos of my family, husband,
and children, to remind me a lot of people love me. My dog
and two cats run around my office, to remind me to play.
Watching my two Siamese fighting fish (a.k.a. Betta fish) swim
around relaxes me. The glass partition separating them keeps
them from destroying each other, reminding me to maintain
an assertive edge! What keepsakes, toys, plants, or reminders
do *you* keep around to boost your productivity? If you don't
have any, get some, stat!

MAINTAINING YOUR ENERGETIC EDGE

The only way the PWF process will work is if you take direct
action to *make* it work. Any change requires you to focus your
efforts on actively producing the changes you want to achieve.
Unfortunately, too many of us seem more interested in thinking good thoughts than in actually taking action.

Unless you've been living in a cave the last few years, you've
certainly heard of "The Secret." This popular philosophy pur-
ports to relate the true secret of success in all aspects of life.
It's all about optimistic thinking and a faith in abundance; that

is, a belief the Universe will provide for you, assuming you believe in whatever it is you really want.

The Secret is often interpreted to mean that all you have to do is wish really hard for good things to happen, and they will. To be fair, though, I believe that many of the people who've adopted the philosophy have misinterpreted it. I think The Secret is really a reminder of the value of positive thinking and self-belief. There's nothing wrong with either; in fact, they're necessary ingredients to any success.

But let's face it: You can't hope things into existence just by thinking good thoughts about them. True productivity requires action. You have to jump into your work with both feet, facing the challenges between you and your goals and dealing with them in a proactive way. As the saying goes, motion always beats meditation—assuming you've done your homework and thought about the potential outcomes.

So use your intelligence, energy, and problem-solving skills to grab hold of any tools available, and use them to get the job done. And always, always, keep your eyes open to the possibilities!

If you combine positive visualization with positive action, the productivity that results will bring you the things you want. *You* will solve the problem, not magical thinking. But if you just sit there and dream without applying your physical energy to what you want to accomplish, you're wasting your time and talent, and nothing productive will ever happen.

Run Past the Base!

When you do put your energy into action, give it your all. Some may think this statement contradicts my mantra to reduce, reduce, reduce, but I don't think so. What I'm telling you here is not to work harder or longer, but to focus your energy like a laser. Don't make a half-effort at getting something important done. Stay focused to ensure it *does* get done, and don't give up too soon.

A while back, I was watching my son James at baseball prac-

🕐 While working on a critical task, give it 110 percent of
your energy and focus, so you don't undershoot the mark.
That way, you won't have to waste time doing it over.

tice, and the coach was teaching the nine-year-olds to "run
past the base"—to pretend the base was actually ten feet *past*
the base. When I ran track in high school, the coach taught us
to "run past the finish." At the Indy 500, you can bet the cars
don't slow down as they near the checkered flag—they speed
up and go as fast as possible.

In other words, you can't just stop when you hit your goal,
because you would have to slow down as you near it. Instead,
pretend your goal is farther away than the endpoint, whatever
that looks like for you. You can't ease up as you near the base,
the tape, or the finish line. Pretend there's a dragon breathing fire down your back. Don't get lazy or slow down just
when your greatest efforts are required and count the most.
As Olympic contenders who have lost the gold by a few hun-
dredths of a second know, you can't win if you let up. So stay in
the lead and run past the base, giving it your all!

SUMMARY: PWF STEP 6 CHECKUP

Establishing and maintaining an effective workflow routine
isn't enough. You have to power it with your personal energy,
constantly and reliably, or everything falls apart.

Managing your capacity is central to the entire PWF process. To be productive, you must have the capacity to do so. So
focus on the physical factors affecting your energy: sleep, diet,
exercise, and your own happiness. Take care of yourself, so
your workflow engine stays up and running with a minimum
of fuss. You can't prevent every potential "power outage," but
you can prevent most of them if you'll try.

First, take steps to reduce your energy expenditure. Your personal "battery" has only so much capacity, so learn to work within your limits and recharge whenever necessary. Overwork will drain you so far you won't be able to get anything done productively. When possible, take your meal breaks, rest breaks, weekends, and vacations—or you'll pay for it with flagging energy and mental strain.

Be sure to get plenty of sleep, too; it reduces stress, evens out your biochemistry, allows your muscles to restore themselves, and gives your brain time to process and deal with new information. Implement simple actions to keep your sleep schedule steady: control the thermostat, shut out snoring, take power naps when necessary, and keep your bedroom sleep-related.

You also need to watch your diet, focusing on portion control and making sure you eat foods that boost your energy rather than drag you down. Add exercise to your daily routine, whether you maintain a regular workout schedule or sneak in "subversive exercise" like taking the stairs instead of the elevator, parking at the far end of the parking lot so you can walk farther, or watching TV from a treadmill.

Don't leave your mental health out of the equation! Do everything you can think of to make yourself happier. For example:

- Make empowered choices.
- Spend more time with your family.
- Do something nice for someone else.
- Laugh at adversity.
- Surround yourself with happy things.

The PWF will work for you only if you focus on making it work. Step up and make every effort you can to maintain your energetic edge, so your workflow process will keep running without a hitch.

A Final Note

One of the reasons that Scott Adams's cartoon *Dilbert* is so popular is that it wryly captures precisely what American office workers experience and feel on a daily basis. The above quote, attributed to evil HR Director Catbert, resonates with those who feel overworked, put-upon, and stretched thin— especially during this time of economic downturn.

As I write this in November 2011, we're still mired in the Great Recession, although some government analysts would say otherwise. Productivity is down and the job market is tighter than it's been in decades, which means that most of us are willing to do whatever it takes to keep the jobs we have. Fear is often a great motivator. People work ridiculously long hours in a desperate attempt to maximize productivity, no matter what, because they're afraid of losing their jobs in a down economy without the reassurance of getting another one.

Sadly, this often ends up hurting us more than it helps. Given our temporal constraints, life must be a series of trade-offs; when you say yes to one thing, you have to say no to another. One of the worst things about working long hours is that it keeps you away from friends and loved ones. Absence may make the heart grow fonder, but only up to a certain point; you have to spend time with those you care for, so you can maintain and develop your relationships. Your children especially need you, at least as a positive role model.

Furthermore, many busy people push taking care of themselves down to the bottom of their to-do lists, where it often falls off and becomes lost in the daily triage of time management. This is bad enough, but too much work also results in exhaustion, which in the short term causes mistakes and rework, resulting in even lower productivity.

In the long term, excessive overtime can have detrimental effects on your health. *Karoshi* (death from overwork) has been an accepted concept in Japan for decades, though it's difficult to recognize in most other countries, which don't keep statistics for such things. Depression is also common among the overworked, and the suicide rate is higher among the chronically depressed. Feeling that you're forced to put in too many hours, for whatever reason, can make you feel trapped and helpless. These mental stresses, when added to the physical ones, can result, one way or another, in a catastrophic breakdown.

Remember this: You're not a machine, so don't try to be one. A decent work-life balance and plenty of rest are required for any human being to thrive productively. The true bottom line is that it's in your best interest, and your company's, for you to trim the fat out of your schedule and tame the beast of overwork. You can't be successfully productive if you work yourself into the hospital . . . or an early grave.

AN EXTRA HOUR—OR MORE

As you may recall, one of my promises associated with the PWF is that if you put it into play, you can tweak your productivity enough to clear an extra ninety minutes a day from your work schedule. That begs a question: What would you do with that extra time?

In July 2011, I asked my followers on LinkedIn what they would do with an extra hour in their day. Of the five possible choices, the one that attracted the most votes was "Leisure time with family and friends," a choice I most heartily approve of. It took 40 percent of the 140 votes, nearly twice as many as the runner-up, "Work out, go to the gym" (22 percent), which is also a great choice. "Sleep" and "Other" each pulled down

15 percent of the vote, with only 8 percent of the respondents opting for more work.

Fifteen individuals who selected "Other" expanded on their answers in the Comments. Some preferred to maintain a balance of all the things they were already doing, spreading the extra hour over various categories, while others wanted to read more, write more, increase their volunteer efforts, take dancing and art classes, learn a foreign language, go for walks, meditate, or otherwise unwind.

I was happy to see that most of my voters would elect to take care of themselves more if they had just a little more time in the day. This desire—no, this *need*—to have more time off is consistent across gender, age, and nationality. My poll provided a quick snapshot of what busy office workers are experiencing. From the hundreds of talks and consultations I've done on the past twenty years, I know that most people are, in fact, sick to death of trying to do more with less. What they really need is a system that lets them do less while accomplishing more. That's what I'm offering with the PWF system, if you're willing to take me up on it.

Or would you rather stay shackled to your desk? Sadly, some people would, because they're addicted to the stresses and strains of work. Just as alcohol consumes the alcoholic, work consumes the workaholic. Do you want to be on call, twenty-four hours a day, for the rest of your life? If so, then you need the PWF system more than most.

Too Much for Too Little

Speaking of shackles: In his book *Chained to the Desk: A Guidebook for Workaholics, Their Partners and Children, and the Clinicians Who Treat Them*, psychotherapist Bryan Robinson depicts workaholism as "an obsessive-compulsive disorder that manifests itself through self-imposed demands, an inability to regulate work habits, and an over-indulgence in work to the exclusion of most other life activities." According to Robinson, workaholism is "the best-dressed problem of the twenty-first century." (It still is, well into the twenty-first.)

As Tony Schwartz, author of *What Really Matters: Searching for Wisdom in America*, points out, "Any culture inevitably pulls people toward its norms. Ours elevates those who work relentlessly and disdains those who are more laid-back. . . . Those who embrace long hours and devotion to the workplace not only earn a special place in the ranks of the company, but they also frequently earn more money—which translates into even more approval in our culture."

But nothing comes for free. Workaholism has severe consequences as well as rewards. To name just a few: workaholism is one of the chief causes of divorce, according to a survey by the American Academy of Matrimonial Lawyers; and research shows that the children of workaholics suffer notably higher rates of anxiety and depression than the children of ordinary workers.[33] Workaholics are also more self-destructive than most people: they're much more likely to abuse alcohol; they endure more stress-related ailments; and they have more have extramarital affairs (which can't help that divorce rate any).

On top of all that, what happens when you kill yourself for all those years and then get the pink slip? Don't fool yourself—it's happening more and more often these days, as corporate loyalty to employees increasingly goes out the window in the face of economic necessity. So when it does happen, what's left? When you come out of your self-induced eighty-hour workweek, what shape will your relationships be in? Will you have any friends left? What about family? And how will you deal with the health problems resulting from a severe lack of taking care of yourself?

Is this really the kind of future you want to face?

If you're not there yet, there's still time to halt this nightmare scenario right in its tracks. Rather than ruin your health, alienate your family and friends, and lose yourself, take steps to nip workaholism in the bud right now, while you still can. Pull back. Weed out the unnecessary and trivial. It requires self-discipline and a willingness to put yourself and the things that truly matter to you first rather than last. Clearly, you have plenty of self-discipline; otherwise you wouldn't be working so many hours. Making yourself a priority is probably a bigger problem. But it's worth trying, because implementing the workflow formula that I've described in this book will make life a lot easier for you by freeing up valuable recharge time without forcing you to sacrifice one jot of productivity.

Admit it—deep down, wouldn't you love to have a little more time for yourself and your family, especially if your productivity didn't suffer? If you could keep your boss happy without driving yourself into the ground, wouldn't you? Well, you've got the tools for doing that right here in these pages. You don't have to put them all into practice at once. You can start slowly, and then ratchet up your commitment incrementally as you start to see results. And you will. Eventually, you'll recover that extra hour a day (or more) that my poll respondents spoke of so longingly.

Enough Said

They say hard work is good for the soul, and it can certainly help you get ahead. But as with anything, moderation is the key here. Too much work can keep you away from what really matters to you. It can also cause both physical and mental stress, which can have devastating health effects.

Keep all that from happening. Give the Productivity Workflow Formula a try. You've got absolutely nothing to lose—and a whole new productive lease on life to gain.

Go to www.LauraStack.com/WhatToDo to receive complimentary bonus material, tip sheets, and group discussion worksheets.

Go to www.bkconnection.com/whattodo-sa to assess your strengths and improvement opportunities around your PWF.

THE PRODUCTIVITY WORKFLOW
FORMULA (PWF) SELF-ASSESSMENT

To help you assess yourself in the six steps of the PWF and create your individual action plan, I've created a self-assessment to test your strengths and improvement opportunities. This online companion product is available at www.bkconnection .com/whattodo-sa. Your results will also include an interpretation of your score and tips. You may print your results, forward them to others, and have others take the test to assess you.

Bulk-order discounts are available for teams, book clubs, and organizations.

NOTES

1. "The Great Prosperity, 1949–1979; The Great Regression, 1980–Now," *New York Times*, September 4, 2011. Also based on information from Robert B. Reich, University of California, Berkeley; "The State of Working America" by the Economic Policy Institute; Thomas Piketty, Paris School of Economics, and Emmanuel Saez, University of California, Berkeley; the U.S. Census Bureau; the U.S. Bureau of Labor Statistics; and the Federal Reserve.

2. "Productivity and Costs: Second Quarter 2011, Preliminary," news release, U.S. Bureau of Labor Statistics, August 9, 2011.

3. "Second Quarter 2011 Productivity Growth Revised Downward," The Editor's Desk, U.S. Bureau of Labor Statistics, September 9, 2011.

4. "The Great Prosperity, 1949–1979; The Great Regression, 1980–Now," *New York Times*, September 4, 2011. Also based on information from Robert B. Reich, University of California, Berkeley; "The State of Working America" by the Economic Policy Institute; Thomas Piketty, Paris School of Economics, and Emmanuel Saez, University of California, Berkeley; the U.S. Census Bureau; the U.S. Bureau of Labor Statistics; and the Federal Reserve.

5. Randolph H. Thomas, "Effects of Scheduled Overtime on Labor Productivity," *Journal of Construction Engineering and Management*, 118, no. 1 (March 1992).; Todd Dawson, Anneke Heitmann, and Alex Kerin, "Industry Trends, Costs and Management of Long Working Hours," extended abstract from the conference Long Working Hours, Safety, and Health: Toward a National Research Agenda, University of Maryland, Baltimore, Maryland, April 29–30, 2004, at http://www.cdc.gov/niosh/topics/workschedules/abstracts/dawson.html; and J. Nevison, *White Collar Project Management Questionnaire Report* (Concord, Mass.: Oak Associates, 1992).

6. "Americans Waste More Than 2 Hours a Day at Work, Costing Companies $759 Billion a Year, According to Salary.Com and America Online Survey," press release, Salary.com. Online at http://www.salary.com/sitesearch/layoutscripts/sisl_display.asp?filename=

&path=/destinationsearch/par485_body.html; and "The Top Office Time-Wasters," Boston.com, undated, at http://www.boston.com/business/gallery/wastingtimeatwork?pg=2.

7. "Workers Think 'Water Cooler' Talk Improved Productivity," *Central Valley Business Times*, June 21, 2006; Maggie Reed, "Water Cooler Chatter: Is It Discussion or Distraction?" *The Network Journal* (September 2006); and "Discussion or Distraction?" OfficeTeam news release, June 2006, at http://officeteam.rhi.mediaroom.com/index.php?s=247&item=815.

8. See http://www.theproductivitypro.com/r_free_stuff.htm.

9. See www.domoregreatwork.com.

10. Richard Holmes, *The Oxford Companion to Military History* (Oxford and New York: Oxford University Press, 2001).

11. Jonathan B. Spira and Joshua B. Feintuch, "The Cost of Not Paying Attention: How Interactions Impact Knowledge Worker Productivity," Basex, Inc., September 2005, at http://www.basex.com/web/tbghome.nsf/23e5e39594c064ee852564ae004fa010/ea4eae82 8bd411be8525742f0006cde3/$FILE/CostOfNotPayingAttention .BasexReport.pdf.

12. See, for example, the products at www.cubedoor.com.

13. C. M. Conway and M. H. Christiansen, "Statistical Learning Within and Between Modalities: Pitting Abstract Against Stimulus Specific Representations," *Psychological Science* 17 (2006): 905–912.

14. Joshua S. Rubinstein, David E. Meyer, and Jeffrey E. Evans, "Executive Control of Cognitive Processes in Task Switching," *Journal of Experimental Psychology: Human Perception and Performance* 27, no. 4 (2001): 763–797.

15. "National Safety Council Estimates That at Least 1.6 Million Crashes Each Year Involve Drivers Using Cell Phones and Texting," press release, National Safety Council, January 12, 2010 (revised 2011), at http://www.nsc.org/Pages/NSCestimates16millioncrashes causedbydriversusingcellphonesandtexting.aspx.

16. See http://www.daytimer.com/laurastack.

17. See "25 Fantastic To-Do List Apps for iPhone," at http://iphone.appstorm.net/roundups/productivity-roundups/25-fantastic-to-do-list-apps-for-iphone/.

18. "Julian Treasure: The 4 Ways Sounds Affect Us," TED Talk, 2009, at http://www.ted.com/talks/julian_treasure_the_4_ways_sound_affects_us.html.

19. Greg R. Oldham, Anne Cummings, Leann J. Mischel, James M. Schmidtke, and Jing Zhou, "Can Personal Stereos Improve

Productivity?" *HR Magazine* 41 (1996): 95–99, at http://findarticles
.com/p/articles/mi_m3495/is_n4_v41/ai_18298711; and Teresa Le-
siuk, "The Effect of Music Listening on Work Performance," *Psychology of Music* 33, no. 2 (2005): 173–191.

20. See http://www.TheProductivityPro.com/Outlook.

21. To download a detailed manual with screen shots and step-
by-step instructions, go to www.TheProductivityPro.com/download
.htm.

22. Harry E. Chambers, *My Way or the Highway: The Micromanagement Survival Guide* (San Francisco: Berrett-Koehler Publishers,
2004).

23. Paul Gompers, Anna Kovner, Josh Lerner, and David Sharf-
stein, "Performance Persistence in Entrepreneurship," Harvard
Business School Working Paper 09-028 (2008); and Paul A. Gompers, Josh Lerner, David Scharfstein, and Anna Kovner, "Performance
Persistence in Entrepreneurship," *Journal of Financial Economics* 96
(2010): 18–32.

24. Mika Kivimäki, G. David Batty, Mark Hamer, Jane E. Fer-
rie, Jussi Vahtera, Marianna Virtanen, Michael G. Marmot, Archana
Singh-Manoux, and Martin J. Shipley, "Using Additional Information on Working Hours to Predict Coronary Heart Disease: A Co-
hort Study," *Annals of Internal Medicine* 154, no. 7 (2011): 457–463, at
http://www. ncbi.nlm.nih.gov/pubmed/21464347.

25. Scott A. Golder and Michael W. Macy, "Diurnal and Seasonal
Mood Vary with Work, Sleep, and Daylength Across Diverse Cul-
tures," *Science* 333, no. 6051 (September 30, 2011): 1878–1881.

26. Matthew P. Walker, Tiffany Brakefield, Alexandra Morgan,
J. Allan Hobson, and Robert Stickgold, "Practice with Sleep Makes
Perfect: Sleep-Dependent Motor Skill Learning," *Neuron* 35 (2002):
205–211.

27. See "Research on Drowsy Driving" at http:// www.nhtsa.gov/
Driving+Safety/Distracted+Driving/Research+on+Drowsy+
Driving; and NCSDR/NHTSA Expert Panel on Driver Fatigue and
Sleepiness (undated), "Drowsy Driving and Automobile Crashes," at
http://www.nhtsa.gov/people/injury/drowsy_driving1/Drowsy.html.

28. F.P. Cappuccio, F.M. Taggart, N.-B. Kandala, A. Currie,
E. Peile, S. Stranges, and M.A. Miller, "Meta-Analysis of Short
Sleep Duration and Obesity in Children, Adolescents and Adults,"
Sleep 31, no. 5 (2008): 619–626; University of Warwick, "Sleep De-
privation Doubles Risks of Obesity in Both Children and Adults,"
ScienceDaily (2006), retrieved November 14, 2011, at http://www

.sciencedaily.com/releases/2006/07/060713081140.htm; Karine Spiegel, Esra Tasali, Plamen Penev, and Eve Van Cauter, "Brief Communication: Sleep Curtailment in Healthy Young Men Is Associated with Decreased Leptin Levels, Elevated Ghrelin Levels, and Increased Hunger and Appetite," *Annals of Internal Medicine* 141, no. 11 (2004): 846–850; and S. Taheri, L. Lin, D. Austin, T. Young, and E. Mignot, "Short Sleep Duration Is Associated with Reduced Leptin, Elevated Ghrelin, and Increased Body Mass Index," *PLoS Medicine* 1, no. 3 (2004): e62, doi:10.1371/journal.pmed.0010062, at http://www.plosmedicine.org/article/info%3Adoi%2F10.1371%2Fjournal.pmed.0010062.

29. Sara C. Mednick, Ken Nakayama, Jose L. Cantero, Mercedes Atienza, Alicia A. Levin, Neha Pathak, and Robert Stickgold, "The Restorative Effect of Naps on Perceptual Deterioration," *Nature Neuroscience* 5, no. 7 (July 2002): 677–681.

30. Brian Wansink, James E. Painter, and Yeon-Kyung Lee, "The Office Candy Dish: Proximity's Influence on Estimated and Actual Consumption," *International Journal of Obesity* 30, no. 5 (May 2006), 871–875.

31. B.J. Rolls, L.S. Roe, and J.S. Meengs, "Salad and Satiety: Energy Density and Portion Size of a First Course Salad Affect Energy Intake at Lunch," *Journal of the American Dietetic Association* 104 (2004): 1570–1576.

32. Allan Luks, "Helper's High: Volunteering Makes People Feel Good, Physically and Emotionally," *Psychology Today* (October 1988).

33. Claudia Flowers, "Workaholics Tend to Be Married to the Job—and Nothing Else," *Charlotte Business Journal*, December 20, 1999.

INDEX

Adams, Scott, 162
availability caching, 48, 59

Bennett, J. Michael, 93
blacklists, for e-mail addresses,
  90, 113
bottlenecks in workflow, eliminating, 126–130, 139
Boyd, Montague L., 5
breaks, value of taking, 144–146

caching concept, 48
cell phones, car accidents caused
  by using, 68
Chained to the Desk (Robinson),
  164
choosing correctly, three-step
  process of, 58–59, 60
Christiansen, Morten, 66
communication skills, 115,
  117–123, 139
complaining, negative impact
  of, 21
Conway, Christopher, 66
coworkers: demands on your
  time by, 11, 17; distractions
  caused by, 62–64; time
  wasted by socializing with,
  20–21, 36, 81–83, 87
customer relationship management (CRM) software, 29,
  97, 106

deadlines, management of, 41
decision-making, 57–59, 60
decision tree for managing
  e-mail, 111–112
delegating tasks, 41, 102–103
diet, importance of good, 151–
  153, 160, 161
digital media. *See* electronic
  media
distractions at work, 18–23, 36,
  61–62, 85–87; electronic
  media as source of, 18–19,
  36, 74–77, 87; external, 62–
  64, 86–87; internal, 65–72,
  87; noise as source of, 64,
  81–83, 87; socializing as
  source of, 20–21, 36, 81–83,
  87
Do More Great Work (Stanier),
  24
Drucker, Peter, 25

electronic media: information
  management using, 106;
  as source of distractions at
  work, 18–19, 36, 74–77, 87;
  time management using,
  97–100
e-mail: blacklists for, 90, 113;
  decision tree for managing,
  111–112; Microsoft Outlook
  used for, 89–90, 107–110;

Searfoss, Rick, 44
Secret, The (of positive think-
    ing), 158–159
self-management, 18, 37
6-D Information Management
    System, 88, 101, 102–103,
    112, 114; for e-mail, 106–
    112; for paper, 104–105; for
    voicemail, 105–106
sleep, importance of sufficient,
    147–150, 160, 161
smoking, as workplace distrac-
    tion, 23, 36
socializing at work, time wasted
    by, 20–21, 36, 81–83, 87
social media: in personal time
    management system, 97; as
    workplace distraction, 19–20
Stack, Laura: as author, 16, 173;
    father's advice to, 77–78;
    featured in national media,
    173; as Microsoft Certi-
    fied Application Specialist
    (MCAS), 107; as president of
    National Speakers Associa-
    tion, xiii, 44, 173; as produc-
    tivity consultant, ix, 16, 173;
    son of, 134, 159; as speaker,
    xiii, 16, 44, 173
Stanier, Michael Bungay, 24
Start-to-Finish Rule, 101, 104
Superglue Rule, 101, 104

teamwork, importance of,
    130–131, 139

Three-Minute Rule, 101, 104,
    107, 114
tickler files, 95–96, 104, 106,
    108, 109
to-do lists: proliferation of
    items on, 9, 10, 11, 36; tri-
    age system applied to, 31–35.
    See also HIT (High Impact
    Task) lists; Master lists; Not-
    To-Do lists
Tracy, Brian, 50
Treasure, Julian, 81
triage system, applied to to-do
    lists, 31–35, 36, 46, 47, 59
Twain, Mark, 121
Twitter, 19–20, 97

wasting time, main causes of,
    18–23, 35–36
Web. See Internet
What Really Matters (Schwartz),
    165
whitelists, for e-mail addresses,
    90, 113
workaholism, 164–165
workflow: eliminating bottle-
    necks in, 126–130, 139;
    human factors in, 129–131,
    138–139; identifying time-
    wasting procedures in, 132;
    impact of teamwork on,
    130–131, 139; improving
    procedures in, 115–116,
    133–134, 137–138, 139;
    organizing, 116–117

ABOUT THE AUTHOR

Laura Stack, MBA, is the president of The Productivity Pro®, Inc., a consulting firm specializing in productivity improvement in high-stress environments, and the 2011–2012 president of the National Speakers Association (NSA). Her keynotes and seminars focus on increasing profitability by improving output, reducing inefficiency, and saving time in the workplace. Laura is a high-energy, high-content speaker, who educates, entertains, and motivates professionals to improve value and results. She's the recipient of the Certified Speaking Professional (CSP) designation, the NSA's highest earned award for excellence in speaking.

For twenty years, Laura has advised leaders on barriers to employee productivity and implemented productivity-improvement programs at companies such as Walmart, Cisco Systems, UBS Financial Services, Chick-fil-A, KPMG, Lockheed Martin, Aramark, Heinz, and Bank of America. The author of five books, including *SuperCompetent* and *Leave the Office Earlier*, Laura focuses on teaching leaders, professionals, salespeople, and entrepreneurs how to align strategy and execution to achieve Maximum Results in Minimum Time. Her popular monthly electronic newsletter has subscribers in thirty-eight countries. She's represented Microsoft, 3M, Xerox, and Office Depot in spokesperson roles and is the designer of the Productivity Pro planner by Day-Timer.

Widely regarded as one of the leading experts in the field of employee productivity and workplace issues, Laura has been featured nationally on the CBS Early Show, CNN, NPR, Bloomberg, NBC TV, WB News, the *New York Times*, *USA Today*, the *Wall Street Journal*, the *Washington Post*, *O Magazine*, *Entrepreneur*, *Reader's Digest*, and *Forbes* magazine.

Laura lives with her husband and three children in Denver, Colorado.

EDUCATIONAL RESOURCES BY LAURA STACK
AVAILABLE FROM THE PRODUCTIVITY PRO®, INC.

Books

SuperCompetent: The Six Keys to Perform at Your Productive Best

*The Exhaustion Cure: Up Your Energy from Low to Go in
21 Days*

*Find More Time: How to Get Things Done at Home,
Organize Your Life, and Feel Great About It*

*Leave the Office Earlier: How to Do More in Less Time
and Feel Great About It*

Workshops

Maximizing Your Productivity with Technology

SuperCompetent®

What to Do When There's Too Much to Do

How to Concentrate in Distracting Environments

Staying on Top of the Inbox

Organizing Your Office and Your Life

Meetings, Meetings, Meetings: Where Minutes Are Taken
and Hours Are Wasted

Controlling Your Time in an Uncontrollable Workplace

Increasing Sales Through Increased Efficiency

How Leaders Increase Employee Productivity

Online quizzes:
http://www. TheProductivityPro.com/r_quizzes.htm
e-Booklets: http://www. TheProductivityPro.com/t_ebooks.htm
Keynotes: http://www.TheProductivityPro.com/keynotes
Seminars: http://www.TheProductivityPro.com/training
Online Outlook training videos:
http://www.TheProductivityPro.com/Outlook

Licensed training:
http://www.TheProductivityPro.com/t_licensed_training.htm
Multimedia Store:
http://www.TheProductivityPro.com/t_productivity_tools.htm
Pre-Recorded webinars:
http://www.TheProductivityPro.com/s_virtual-webinar.htm
CD sets: http://www.TheProductivityPro.com/t_boxed_sets.htm
MP3s: http://www.TheProductivityPro.com/t_mp3s.htm
DVDs: http://www.TheProductivityPro.com/t_training_dvds.htm
Day-Timer by Laura Stack: http://www.daytimer.com/laurastack
Subscribe to free monthly newsletter:
http://www.TheProductivityPro.com/r_subscribe.htm
**150+ articles for free reprint in your company newsletter
or blog**: http://www.TheProductivityPro.com/articles

Information

To inquire about having Laura Stack speak at your next meeting,
contact:

The Productivity Pro®, Inc.
Phone: 303-471-7401
Laura@TheProductivityPro.com
Web: www.TheProductivityPro.com
www.LauraStack.com
Blog: www.TheProductivityPro.com/blog
Twitter: www.twitter.com/laurastack
Facebook: www.facebook.com/ProductivityPro
LinkedIn: www.linkedin.com/in/laurastack
YouTube: www.youtube.com/theproductivitypro

Berrett–Koehler
Publishers

Berrett-Koehler is an independent publisher dedicated to an ambitious mission: *Creating a World That Works for All.*

We believe that to truly create a better world, action is needed at all levels—individual, organizational, and societal. At the individual level, our publications help people align their lives with their values and with their aspirations for a better world. At the organizational level, our publications promote progressive leadership and management practices, socially responsible approaches to business, and humane and effective organizations. At the societal level, our publications advance social and economic justice, shared prosperity, sustainability, and new solutions to national and global issues.

A major theme of our publications is "Opening Up New Space." Berrett-Koehler titles challenge conventional thinking, introduce new ideas, and foster positive change. Their common quest is changing the underlying beliefs, mindsets, institutions, and structures that keep generating the same cycles of problems, no matter who our leaders are or what improvement programs we adopt.

We strive to practice what we preach—to operate our publishing company in line with the ideas in our books. At the core of our approach is stewardship, which we define as a deep sense of responsibility to administer the company for the benefit of all of our "stakeholder" groups: authors, customers, employees, investors, service providers, and the communities and environment around us.

We are grateful to the thousands of readers, authors, and other friends of the company who consider themselves to be part of the "BK Community." We hope that you, too, will join us in our mission.

A BK Life Book

This book is part of our BK Life series. BK Life books change people's lives. They help individuals improve their lives in ways that are beneficial for the families, organizations, communities, nations, and world in which they live and work. To find out more, visit **www.bk-life.com**.

Berrett–Koehler
Publishers

A community dedicated to creating
a world that works for all

Visit Our Website: www.bkconnection.com

Read book excerpts, see author videos and Internet movies, read
our authors' blogs, join discussion groups, download book apps, find
out about the BK Affiliate Network, browse subject-area libraries of
books, get special discounts, and more!

Subscribe to Our Free E-Newsletter, the *BK Communiqué*

Be the first to hear about new publications, special discount offers,
exclusive articles, news about bestsellers, and more! Get on the list
for our free e-newsletter by going to **www.bkconnection.com**.

Get Quantity Discounts

Berrett-Koehler books are available at quantity discounts for orders
of ten or more copies. Please call us toll-free at (800) 929-2929 or
email us at **bkp.orders@aidcvt.com**.

Join the BK Community

BKcommunity.com is a virtual meeting place where people from
around the world can engage with kindred spirits to create a world
that works for all. BKcommunity.com members may create their own
profiles, blog, start and participate in forums and discussion groups,
post photos and videos, answer surveys, announce and register for
upcoming events, and chat with others online in real time. Please join
the conversation!

MIX
Paper from
responsible sources
FSC
www.fsc.org
FSC® C012752

Certified

Corporation
bcorporation.net